ARCHITECTURE

Complied and Edited by:
Gary Robinson

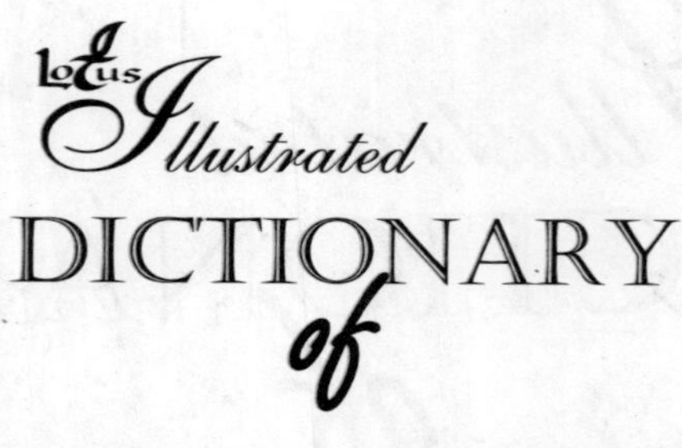

ARCHITECTURE

ISBN 81 89093 12 6

Published by:
Lotus Press Publishers & Distributors
Unit No. 220, 2nd Floor, 4735/22,
Prakash Deep Building, Ansari Road, Darya Ganj,
New Delhi- 110002, Ph.: 32903912, 23280047, 09811838000
• E-mail : lotuspress1984@gmail.com www.lotuspress.co.in

Printed at : Lotus Press Publishers & Distributors, New Delhi

PREFACE

Architecture is the, oldest and most established field of Engineering. At the same time it is an ever-evolving field. Compared to other branches of Engineering such as Mechanical, Electrical, Electronic, and Chemical etc., Architecture directly affects the life of masses. One of the basic needs of Human beings i.e. – Shelter is provided by the virtue of Architecture.

An Architect applies his skills in order to suffice the demands of customer, within available resources, to provide him with his 'dream house'. Apart from homes an Architect plans and develops Railway stations, Airports, Bridges and Flyovers, Public buildings, Office and Trade centres. As an Architect work on such projects his learning never ceases.

But here lies the catch. In order to make this journey of perpetual learning, through experience, more easy, joyful, and sustainable one has to explore many books of great value. As these books contain many specific words, which cannot be understood without the help of a good reference book, it becomes compulsory to possess one.

This dictionary is an attempt to give an access to the whole paraphernalia of Architectural terms in a crisp package. The terms have been explained in simple and comprehensible manner, with relevant pictures and illustrations to bring clarity. The dictionary can be taken as a complete and cognisable set of Architectural terms to be used as a referral. Since Architecture is a vast subject, a complete inventory of the terms can hardly be claimed in one lexicon, but nonetheless, an attempt has been made towards providing a gamut of terms, which form a part and parcel of the subject.

We have taken a very keen architectural approach indesigning this lexicon

■ 'dropping' a stringer

in carpentry, means cutting short on the bottom of a stairs, to allow for thickness of the first tread.

■ a cross vault (or groin)

is formed at the point at which two barrel (tunnel) vaults intersect at right angles.

■ abacus

1. a tablet placed horizontally on the capital of a column, aiding the support of the architrave.
2. flat portion on top of a capital.
3. ancient counting frame made up of small beads threaded on wires for mathematical calculations. It had beads, which counted as 1, others had the value of 10 others, 100. By moving the beads around complicated multiplication and division could be achieved.
4. the flat slab which sits on top of a capital.

■ abacus or impost block

the slab at the top of a capital between the capital and the architectural member above. See **column, pier, other parts of a column or pier capital, shaft, column base.**

■ abbey

1.a monastery where, either monks live, governed by an abbot, or in the case of nuns, governed by an abbess.
2. church that is not a Cathedral but does, or did at one time have monks living there, e.g. Selby Abbey. May have once been a Cathedral, e.g. Bath or Westminster.

■ above grade

the portion of a building that is above ground level.

■ abut

one thing is said to abut another where it touches, but is not actually tied in, this can vary from buildings forming a terrace to a structural member such as a piece of timber the end of which has simply been planted against another part of the structure

■ abutment

1. a solid piece of masonry used to support a projecting part of a structure, for example, the supports that connect a bridge with a river bank.
2. the support structure at either end of an arch or bridge. The intermediary supports are called piers.
3. solid support absorbing the outward thrust of the arch.
4. a masonry pier or wall erected to balance the force of an arch or vault.
5. a reinforcing block or wall of masonry adding support to the great vaults & arches.

■ acanthus

1. a Mediterranean plant. The leaves are thick, fleshy, and scalloped. A

stylisation of the acanthus leaf began in Greek and Roman decoration, especially on the Corinthian capital. See **Corinthian capital.**
2. plant with thick scalloped leaves that often adorn Greek art and architecture. The capital on a Corinthian column is covered with acanthus leaves, a favourite motif of Greek artists.

■ accelerator

any material added to stucco, plaster or mortar which speeds up the natural set.

■ achaeans

also known as the Mycenaeans, this civilisation built independent city-states in the Peloponnese that were characterised by palaces on fortified hilltops.They wrote in the deciphered Linear B script and many fine examples of their gold jewellery are on display at the National Archaeological Museum in Athens. The height of their civilisation was in 1300 BCE. but was in decline by 1100 BCE. with the arrival of the Dorians.

■ acre

43,500 square feet.

■ acropolis

1. the citadel in ancient Greek towns.
2. the highest part of an ancient city.

■ across the grain

the direction at right angles to the length of the fibres and other longitudinal elements of the wood.

■ adaptive reuse

when a structure is returned to a use other than its original. For instance, when a house becomes an office, a warehouse becomes apartments or a grain elevator and mill become a restraint.

■ adhesion

the property of a coating or sealant to bond to the surface to which it is applied.

■ adhesive

a substance used to bond two surfaces together.

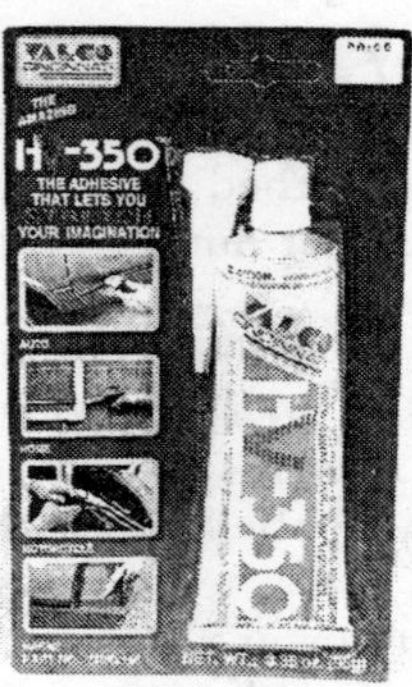

adhesive failure

loss of bond of a coating or sealant from the surface to which it is applied.

aditus

Latin: approach or access, entrance to a place. Entrance to the cavea - according to Vitruvius, 'The entrances (aditus) should be numerous and spacious; those above ought to be unconnected with those below, in a continued line wherever they are, and without turnings; so that when the people are dismissed from the shows, they may not press on one another, but have separate outlets free from obstruction in all parts.' See **precinctiones and vomitoria**

aditus maximus

1. Latin: most important or greatest entrance/access. Roman entrance to the orchestra between the cavea and the scaenae; one on either side of the orchestra; corresponds to the parodos in the Hellenistic theatre ministrative origin.
2. The person or corporate body responsible for gathering together and maintaining a group of documents.

adobe

1. sun-dried brick used in places with warm, dry climates, such as Egypt and Mexico; the clay from which bricks are made; the structures built out of adobe bricks.
2. roughly moulded and sun-dried blocks made from puddled earth reinforced with chopped straw or other fibrous binders, for use in earth-wall construction.

adyton

inner room of a temple.

aggregate

crushed stone, slag or water-worn gravel that comes in a wide range of sizes that is used to surface built-up roofs.

agora

1. Greek: open market or meeting place. Large, open public space which served as a place for assembly for the citizens of a Greek city; the political, civic, religious and commercial centre of a Greek city; buildings for all of these various purposes were constructed as needed in and around the agora.
2. marketplace of a town. It is a Greek term and is used to refer to the forum of a Roman city founded in Greek lands.
3. The word Agora drives from the word *ageiro* meaning *I gather*. In the beginning somebody spoke in an open space and people gathered around. Our modern term *agoraphobia*, meaning fear of public places, comes from this word.
4. often referred to as an ancient marketplace, it was the centre of commercial activity of an ancient city.

5. in ancient Greek architecture, a large open area at the heart of the city whose boundaries are defined by the public buildings that surround it. The 'stoa' and the 'bouleterion' are two of the buildings typically defining the edges of the agora. Agora, Athens.

■ air duct

ducts, usually made of sheet metal, that carry cooled air to all rooms.

■ air filters

adhesive filters made of metal or various fibres that are coated with adhesive liquid to which the particles of lint and dust adhere. These filters will remove as much as 90% of the dirt if they do not become clogged. The more common filters are of the throwaway or disposable type.

■ air infiltration

the amount of air leaking in and out of a building through cracks in walls, windows and doors.

■ air velocity

the velocity of air in the passages between rows of boards in a rack.

■ air-dried lumber

1. lumber that has been piled in yards or sheds for any length of time.

2. timber dried by exposure to air in a yard or shed, without artificial heat.

■ airway

a space between roof insulation and roof boards for movement of air.

■ aisle

1. the space between two arcades or between an arcade and an outer wall.
2. passages flanking the nave and choir, separated from them by arcades.
3. open area of a church parallel to the nave and separated from it by columns or piers. See **nave.**
5. the portion of a church flanking the nave and separated from it by a row of columns or piers.

■ akropolis, acropolis

the Greek word 'akro' means top or high, + 'polis' or city. The sacred precinct in ancient Greek architecture. Today the term is generally reserved for the sacred precinct in Athens.

■ akroterion

decorative element at the apex and both ends of a Pediment.

■ alae

wings off of the atrium of a Roman house.

■ album

a bound volume or book of drawings, prints, photographs, texts, etc., bound as blank pages to which drawings and other media are affixed (compare with *sketchbook*).

■ alligatoring

a condition of paint or aged asphalt brought about by the loss of volatile oils and the oxidation caused by solar radiation. Coarse checking pattern characterised by a slipping of the new paint coating over the old coating to the extent that the old coating can be seen through the fissures. 'Alligatoring' produces a pattern of cracks resembling an alligator hide and is ultimately the result of the limited tolerance of paint or asphalt to thermal expansion or contraction.

■ alloy

a mixture of metals.

■ allure

walkway along the top of a wall.

■ along the grain

the direction parallel with the length of the fibres and other longitudinal elements of the wood.

■ altar

1. in the Roman Church, a table at which the celebration of the Eucharist takes place. It is placed in the most prominent place in the church, usually at the east end, in the choir or sanctuary, facing the main entrance to the church. See **choir, retable.**
2. originally a structure on which offerings to a god were placed, often for sacrifice. In the Christian church, the altar is often in the form of a stone table, can be elaborately carved, and containing relics.
3. the high altar is situated at the east end, in the presbytery.

■ altarpiece

a panel, painted or sculptured, situated above and behind an altar.

alternation of support

a system of supports for an arcade or colonnade in which there are two different types of support. The alternation may be quite obvious, between one pier (strong support) and one column (weak support), or it may exist only in slight differences, such as in the treatment of the shafting on each pier. See **arcade, colonnade, column, pier**

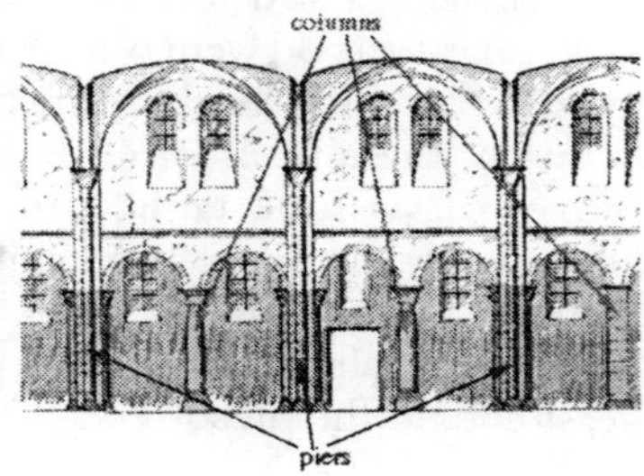

ambo

if there is one speaker's stand in the centre of the front of the church, as is typical in churches with a lecture-hall floor plan, it serves the functions of both lectern and pulpit. The word ambo comes from a Greek word meaning 'both.' In common usage, however, ambos are incorrectly called pulpits.

ambry (or aumbry)

an ambry (or aumbry) is a niche in the wall in a large church. It is generally used for storing various articles that are used in worship.

ambulatory

1. a continuous aisle in a circular building, as in a church.
2. aisle round an apse.
3. a semicircular or polygonal aisle. Usually an ambulatory leads around the east end of the choir; separating the choir from apses or chapels. See **aisle, apse, choir, east end, and hemicycle.**
4. a covered walkway, outdoors (as in a cloister) or indoors; especially the passageway around the apse and the choir (quire) of a church.
5. a roofed passageway, enclosing the apse, and linking the aisles which flank the nave.
6. the ceremonial passageway around the apse, often at a lower level.

amphitheater

from the Greek words 'amphi', on both sides, + 'theatron', the ancient Roman building type used for gladiatorial contests and other entertainments.

One of the best preserved examples of this type is the Flavian amphitheater or 'Colosseum'; an enormous 525'x450' wedge shaped oval, four levels high, seating 50,000 people on raised tiers, each with a good view of the centre of the theatre.

■ **amphora**

1. two - handled jar with a narrow neck and sometimes a tapered base, designed for transporting or storing, olive oil or other liquid, special wine.

■ **analemmata**

Roman: supporting or retaining wall of the theatron; more specifically, exterior wall supporting the cavea

■ **anchor bolt**

1. a device for connecting timber members to concrete or masonry. 2. in residential construction, Bolts to secure a wooden sill plate to concrete, or masonry floor or wall. In commercial construction, Bolts which fasten columns, girders or other members to concrete or masonry such as bolts used to anchor sills to masonry foundation.

■ **ancient**

relating to the historical period beginning with the earliest known civilisations and ending with the fall of the Roman Empire in A.D. 476.

■ **andron**

small, domestic dinning room where men would entertain their friends.

■ **anemometer**

instrument for measuring velocity of airflow.

■ **angle iron**

a piece of iron that forms a right angle and is used to span openings and support masonry at the openings. In brick veneer, they are used to secure the veneer to the foundation. Also known as shelf angle.

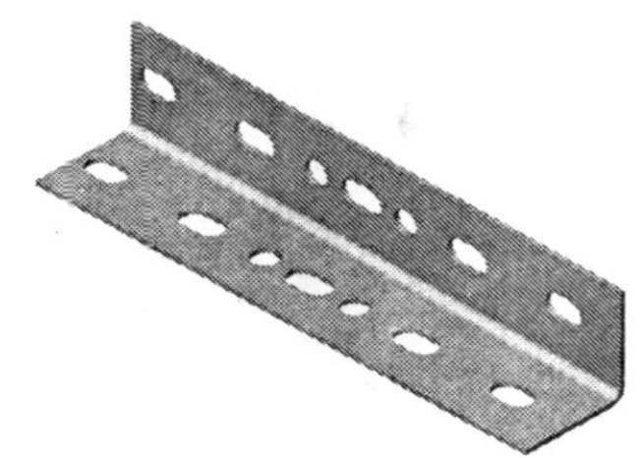

■ **anisotropic**

exhibiting different properties when measured along its different axes.

■ **annealing**

in the manufacturing of float glass, it is the process of controlled cooling done in a lair to prevent residual stresses in the glass. Re-annealing is the process of removing objectionable stresses in glass by re-heating to a suitable temperature followed by controlled cooling.

■ **annulet**

a carved ring encircling a pillar or shaft.

■ **antefix**

the covers at the edges of a roof on all four sides of a building. The cover tiles are the second layer that covers the joints of the first layer of tiles on the roof and end in decorative relief representations.

■ **anthemion leaf**

a leaf from Greek ornamentation found in friezes, column capitals (Corinthian) or cornices.

■ **anticum**

in a Classical temple, an open vestibule before the Cella. Also called Pronaos.

■ **anti-stain chemical**

a chemical applied to timber to prevent or retard chemical or fungal stain development.

■ **anti-walk blocks**

elastomeric blocks that limit lateral glass movement in the glazing channel which may result from thermal, seismic, wind load effects, building movement, and other forces that may apply.

■ **apodyterion**

the change rooms of bath houses See **caldarium, frigidarium, hypocausts, natatio, heliocaminus, laconicum.**

■ **applied force**

see **external force.**

■ **applied or engaged column**

a column which is attached to a wall so that only half of the form projects from the wall. See **column.**

■ **approach**

the area between the sidewalk and the street that leads to a driveway or the transition from the street as you approach a driveway.

■ **apron**

the flat member of the inside trims of a window placed against the wall immediately beneath the stool.

■ **apse**

1. an apse is a rounded alcove behind the altar, particularly in Orthodox churches. In ancient times, when large church buildings were built, they were modelled after a type of Roman public building that had such an alcove.
2. a semicircular area; in most churches it contains the altar.
3. Rounded and usually of a chancel or chapel.
4. a vaulted extension or projection, usually from a choir or chapel and generally circular or polygonal in shape. Contrast with niche.
5. semicircular termination or recess at the end of a church.

■ aqueduct

an engineering structure designed to bring huge quantities of pure water into the city. The u-shaped stone channel that carries the water is at the top of the arcuated structure that is

used to span valleys between the source and the city.

■ arabesque

ornament consisting of garlands of foliage with figures, fancifully interlaced to form graceful curves and painted, inlaid, or carved in low relief.

■ arcade

1. a series of arches supported by columns or piers, or a passageway formed by these arches.
2. row of arches, free-standing and supported on piers or columns; a blind arcade is a 'dummy'.
3. a series of arches supported by columns or piers. Contrast with colonnade See **blind arcade, column, pier, spandrel.**
4. a row of arches set atop piers/ columns. Sometimes refers to the arched roof itself.
5. an open sided covered walkway with a line of arches supported on columns.

■ arcading

an uninterrupted series of arcades

■ arch

1. a curved structure that supports the weight of the material above it.
2. can be round-headed, pointed, two-cantered, or drop; ogee pointed with double curved sides, upper arcs lower concave; lancet pointed formed on an acute-angle triangle; depressed flattened or elliptical; corbelled triangular, peaked, each stone set a little further in until they meet, with a large capstone.
3. a curved structural member spanning an opening or recess. The wedge shaped elements that make up an arch keep one another in place and transform the vertical pressure of the structure above into lateral pressure.
4. a structure usually of wedge-shaped blocks, constructed to span an opening or void in such a way that the downward thrust of the weight above, is converted to an outward movement which is resisted by any suitable means, usually a solid mass of masonry. The

individual wedge- shaped blocks are initially laid on supports, usually timber, called formwork, or cantering. There are a number of different types of arch, the names of which are largely self-explanatory, i.e. elliptical, flat, horseshoe, lancet, obtuse, ogee, segmental, semicircular, triangular.

■ arch or triumphal arch

the ancient Roman commemorative monument in the shape of an arch.
The bas-relief sculpture on the Arch of Constantine depicts his victory over his rival Maxentius, in which he becomes the absolute monarch of the Roman empire.

■ archaeology

someone who studies the physical remains of ancient cultures.

■ archaic period

also known as the Middle Age, it dates from 800 – 480 BC and was marked by the increase in power of the city-states. Due to the decline of the Phoenicians, Greek colonies stretched as far as Africa, Sicily, Italy, southern France, and southern Spain. A Greek alphabet derived from the Phoenician alphabet, Homeric verses, the Olympic Games, and the defeat of the Persians all marked this period.

■ architect

a tradesman who designs and produces plans for buildings, often overseeing the building process.

■ architects rule

1. three sided ruler with different scales on each side. Also referred to as a 'scale.'
2. Any medium that refers to or depicts architectural works, structures, parts of structures, or designs, whether built or unbuilt. Included are textual documents such as specifications and letters; graphic documents such as drawings, prints, and photographs; models; and any other visual media that concern any portion of the built or unbuilt environment. Subjects may include not only architectural works, but also related subjects such as furniture, engineering designs, naval architecture, textiles, architectural ornaments, paper architecture, studies, landscape designs, and stage designs.

■ architectural orders

1. Doric, Ionic, Aeolic, and Corinthian; Doric order: developed on the Greek mainland and in southern Italy and Sicily by 7th century BC; Ionic: developed in Ionia and on some of the Greek islands by the 6th century BC; Aeolic: developed in north-western Asia Minor around the same time but died out by the end of the Archaic period; Corinthian: emerged late in the 5th century BC.

work
2. any subject or built work. It can be a study or a design of a structure, or the representation of a design as depicted on a drawing, model, print, or other medium.

■ **architrave**

1. architectural structure; lintel course of the entablature; horizontal beam resting on the columns of the entablature.
2. the lowest part of an entablature resting on the capital of a column; also, the holdings around a doorway.
3. the lintel or flat horizontal member, which spans the space between columns; in classical architecture, the lowest member of an entablature.
4. the bottom part of the entablature that spans from column to column, upon which the frieze, cornice, and pediment may be found.

■ **archivolt**

one of a series of concentric mouldings on a Romanesque or a Gothic arch.

■ **archivolts**

bands or mouldings (moldings, Am.) surrounding an arched opening. See **jamb, tympanum**

■ **areaway**

an open subsurface space adjacent to a building used to admit light or air or as a means of access to a basement.

■ **armature**

an iron framework in a stained-glass window for supporting larger areas of glass. Introduced in the Gothic period.

■ **arris**

the sharp intersection of two surfaces, e.g. the face and edge of a piece of wood .

■ **arrow loop**

a narrow vertical slit cut into a wall through which arrows could be fired from inside.

■ **art glass**

coloured or ornamental glass used in decorative windows.

■ **(art history)**

someone who studies the art and artists of previous eras.

■ **articulation**

to articulate is 'to divide into meaningful parts'. In architecture, this is a way of expressing the small parts that make up a large building so that it may be understood, in particular, in its relationship to the human body.

■ **aryballos**

perfume pot, usually made of pottery. These vessels were often in the shape of a fantasy creature or a real animal, such as a monkey or a hedgehog

■ **ashlar**

1. stones hewn and squared for use in building, as distinguished from rough stones.
2. squared blocks of smooth stone neatly trimmed to shape.
3. worked stone with flat surface, usually of regular shape and square edges.

■ **ashlar masonry**

stone masonry cut into rectangles and laid to create a wall.

■ **asklepion**

religious sanctuary and Healing centre dedicated to Asklepios, the god of medicine.

■ **asphalt**

a dark brown to black, highly viscous, hydrocarbon produced from the residue left after the distillation of petroleum. Asphalt is used on roofs and highways as a waterproofing agent. Most native asphalt is a residue from evaporated petroleum. It is insoluble in water but soluble in gave. Line when heated. Used widely in building for waterproofing roof coverings of many types, exterior wall coverings, flooring tile, and the like.

■ **astragal**

1. a molding. A simple convex, semicircle molding.
2. a molding, attached to one of a pair of swinging doors, against which the other door strikes.

■ **atlantes**

carved male figure used as a column in classical architecture.

■ **atrium**

1. in an ancient Roman structure, a central room open to the sky, usually having a pool for the collection of rainwater. In Christian churches, a courtyard flanked by porticos.
2. an open courtyard at the entrance of a church, usually surrounded by covered aisles. The atrium of the Early Christian church was originally a place for the catechumens to wait during the celebration of the Eucharist.
3. the main room of a Roman house out of which one had access to other parts of the house. There were many types including ones that were completely roofed (*testudinate*), ones with openings to the sky (*compluvium*), which had, underneath the openings in the house floor, as small rectangular depression to catch rainwater (*impluvium*).

4. atrium In an ancient Roman house, the central courtyard. Today, an atrium may be covered with glass rather than open to the sky.

■ attic

1. the part of the entablature above the cornice, serving to hide the roof.
2. a low wall at the top of the Entablature that hides the roof.

■ attic base

the base of an Ionic column, which consists of two convex mouldings, the top one being smaller, separated by a concave moulding.

■ attic base

the base of an Ionic column, which consists of two convex mouldings, the top one being smaller, separated by a concave moulding.

■ attic story

the portion of the building constructed above the cornice.

■ attic ventilators

in houses, screened opening provided to ventilate an attic space. They are located in the soffit area as inlet ventilators and in the gable end or along the ridge as outlet ventilators. They can also consist of power-driven fans used as an exhaust system. See **louver.**

■ attribute

1. a characteristic of an action or production stage in information processing, such as a kiln number or a log grade.
2. an object or objects closely associated with or belonging to a specific person or character.

■ auger

in carpentry, a wood-boring tool used by a carpenter to bore holes

■ aula regia

Latin: inner court or hall of a king - also 'valva regia' or 'door of a king' used to refer to the main, central entrance to the stage in the Hellenistic theatre; also known as the 'king's or royal door'; corresponds to the porta reggia of the Roman theatre.

■ aulaeum

Latin: theatre curtain - pl. aulaea Roman curtain; curtain could be lowered into the stage, (aulaea premuntur, 'the curtain is let down,' when the play begins); and (aulaeum tollitur, 'the play is ended.')

■ aumbry

1. recess to hold sacred vessels; typically in a chapel.
2. a small recess or cupboard used to hold sacred vessels, most often in the thickness of the wall.
see **authority control.**

■ awnings

a screen of material (such as fabric, plastic or glass), installed over windows and doors to provide shade, protection form the elements and reduce sun exposure to interior spaces.

■ axial coordinates

the system of the ancient Romans for the placement of buildings and roads that uses parallel and perpendicular lines in an even spacing. Also called a grid pattern.

■ axial force

a system of internal forces whose resultant is a force acting along the longitudinal axis of a structural member or assembly.

■ back bar

a work surface with cabinets found in saloons and barbershops.

■ back nailing

the practice of nailing roofing felts to the deck under the overlap, in addition to hot mopping, to prevent slippage of felts.

■ back sawn timber

timber sawn so that the growth rings are inclined at less than 45 degrees to the wide face.

■ backer rod

in glazing, a polyethylene or polyurethane foam material installed under compression and used to control sealant joint depth, provide a surface for sealant tooling, serve as a bond breaker to prevent three-sided adhesion, and provide an hour-glass contour of the finished bead.

■ backfill

filling in any previously excavated area, i.e., The replacement of excavated earth into a trench around and against a basement foundation.. In carpentry, the process of fastening together two pieces of board by gluing blocks of wood in the interior angle.

■ backflow

the flow of liquids through irrigation into the pipes of a potable or drinking water supply from any source which is opposite to the intended direction of flow.

■ backflow preventer

a device or means to prevent backflow into the potable water supply.

■ backhand

a simple molding sometimes used around the outer edge of plain rectangular casing as a decorative feature.

■ backhoe

self-powered excavation equipment that digs by pulling a boom mounted bucket towards itself. It is used to dig basements and/or footings and to install drainage or sewer systems.

■ baffle

a rigid or flexible barrier used to direct and control the flow of air.

■ bailey

1. the ward or courtyard inside the castle walls, includes exercise area, parade ground, emergency corral.
2. castle courtyard and surrounding buildings.

■ balance and /or symmetry

is a concept based on the idea that an object is balanced or symmetrical if it can be cut or divided in two half's with each half being a mirror of the other half.

■ baldachin

1. a stone or marble structure built in the form of a canopy; ornamented canopy supported by columns or suspended from a roof or projected from a wall; a covering (usually of cloth) that serves as a roof to shelter an area from the weather; example as seen in the Greco-Roman theatre at Miletus, Turkey.

■ ball flower

1. characteristic of the Decorated period, these decorative flowers are three petalled and enclose small balls.
2. a globular motif often used in concave moldings of English Gothic architecture. It looks like a flower with three (or sometimes four) petals nearly closed over a central ball. See **also other repetitive decorative motifs**

■ balloon framing

in carpentry, the lightest and most economical form of construction, in which the studding and corner plates are set up in continuous lengths from the first floor line or sill to the roof plate to which all floor joists are fastened.

■ baluster

a small column.

■ balusters

usually small vertical members in a railing used between a top rail and the stair treads or a bottom rail.

■ balustrade

1. a railing, as along a path or stairway.
2. the rails along a porch or balcony.
3. a railing made up of balusters, top rail, and sometimes bottom rail, used on the edge of stairs, teal conies, and porches.

■ baptismal font or font

a receptacle for water, used for baptism. See **baptistery.**

■ baptistery

1. a building or part of a church used for baptism. See **font.**
2. Building used for the baptismal rite and containing the font. Sometimes merely a bay or chapel reserved for baptisms.

■ bar hole

horizontal hole for timber bar used as a door-bolt.

■ bar tracery

tracery, which is, composed of thin stone elements rather than thick ones as in plate tracery. The glass rather than the stone dominates when bar tracery is used. It gives a more delicate, web-like effect.

■ barbed quatrefoil

a four-lobed geometrical motif with a triangular projection at the intersection of two adjacent foils. Compare with cinqfoil, trefoil, quatrefoil bas-relief or low relief Sculpture in which the carved forms project only slightly from the background.

■ barbican

1. an outwork from which the gateway or entrance to a castle was defended.
2. the gateway or outworks defending the drawbridge.

■ barge board

1. a decorative board covering the projecting rafter (fly rafter) of the gable end. At the cornice, this member is a facie board.
2. the vertical-face board set back under the roof edge of a gable, often with decoration.

■ baroque

a style that flourished in the seventeenth and eighteenth centuries, characterised by exuberant decoration, curvaceous forms, and a grand scale generating a sense of movement; later developments show greater restraint.

■ barrel or tunnel vault

semi cylindrical in cross section, is in effect a deep arch or an uninterrupted series of arches, one behind the other, over an oblong space.

■ barrel roof

1. like a covered wagon, or inverted ship; barrel vault is a plain vault of uniform cross-section.
2. a roof design, which in cross section is arched.

■ barrel vault

cylindrical roof.

■ barrel vault or tunnel vault

the simplest form of a vault, consisting of a continuous surface of semicircular or pointed sections. It resembles a barrel or tunnel, which has been cut in half lengthwise.

■ bartizan

1. an overhanging battlemented corner turret, corbelled out; sometimes as grandiose as an overhanging gallery; common in Scotland and France.

■ bas relief

'bas', pronounced 'BA' means

low, therefore a sculpture that is shallow in dimension compared with one that is fully three-dimensional.

■ base

the architectural element on which a column or pier rests.

■ base (or Baseboard)

a board placed against the wall around a room next to the floor to finish properly between floor and plaster.

■ base flashing

the upturned edge of the watertight membrane formed at a roof termination point by the extension of the felts vertically over the cant strip and up the wall for a varying distance where they are secured with mechanical fasteners.

■ base molding

molding used to trim the upper edge of interior baseboard.

■ base ply

an asphalt-saturated and/or coated felt installed as the first ply with 4 inch laps in a built-up roof system under the following felts which can be installed in a shingle-like fashion.

■ base shoe

molding used next to the floor on interior base board. Sometimes called a carpet strip.

■ basilica

1. the early Greek name for a royal palace; a large oblong building with double columns and a semicircular apse at one end, frequently used by Christian emperors of Rome for religious purposes.
2. an important Roman building type consisting of a large central hall often flanked by side aisles. There were many variations.
3. in ancient Roman architecture, a large meeting hall most often used for the law courts. The basilica could also contain the stock exchange, business and offices administrative offices, and therefore was a physical link between law and business.

There are two very different formal expressions of the basilica, illustrated by the earlier Basilica Ulpia or Trajan's Basilica, and the later Basilica of Maxentius and Constantine.

The roof of the trabeated structural system in Trajan's Basilica is supported by many interior columns thus breaking the large space (182' x 450') into smaller sections.

The Basilica of Constantine had an enormous arcuated system (200'x300') of barrel and groin vaults. It carried the thrust of the vaults on piers, and relied on massive buttressing.

■ bastion

1. a solid masonry projection.
2. a small tower at the end of a curtain wall or in the middle of the outside wall; solid masonry projection; structural rather than inhabitable.

■ batch

in drying, a group of timber with similar drying and product characteristics.

■ baths, public

in ancient Roman architecture, this structure combined public baths, gymnasium, exercise yards, stadium shops, libraries and meeting rooms. Natural light entered through clerestory windows in the ends of the barrel-vaulted roofs. It was a masterpiece of engineering providing and disposing of clean water of various temperatures for up to 1600 bathers on a daily basis.

■ batt insulation

strips of insulation, usually fibreglass that fit between studs or other framing.

■ batten

narrow strips of wood used to cover joints or as decorative vertical members over plywood or wide boards.

■ batten plate

a formed piece of metal designed to cover the joint between two lengths of metal edge.

■ batter

1. a sloping part of a curtain wall. The sharp angle at the base of all walls and towers along their exterior surface; talus.
2. an inclined face of wall; hence battered.

■ batter board

one of a pair of horizontal boards nailed to posts set at the corners of an excavation, used to indicate the desired level, also as a fastening for stretched strings to indicate outlines of foundation walls.

battered column

a column that has an inclined or tilted surface with the result of the column being wider at the bottom than at the top.

battlement

1. parapet with indentations or embrasures, with raised portions (merlons) between; crenelations; a narrow wall built along the outer edge of the wall walk for protection against attack.
2. the notched top of a defensive wall.
3. A parapet that alternates between open and solid parts and was originally used on forts and fortresses for defensive purposes.

bauhaus

the style of the Bauhaus School, founded in Germany by Walter Gropius in 1919, emphasising simplicity, functionalism, and craftsmanship.

bay

1. internal division of building marked by roof principals or vaulting piers.
2. a unit of interior space in a building, marked off by architectural divisions.
3. compartment or unit of division of an interior or of a facade - usually between one window or pillar and the next.
4. a subdivision of the interior space of a building. In Romanesque and Gothic churches, the transverse arches and piers of the arcade divide the building into bays.
5. a section of a structure usually containing a door or a window

bay window

1. a projection from a wall containing a window.
2. these windows project out from the front or side of a house. Bay windows have sharp angles and rise up from the ground on the first floor.
3. any window space projecting outward from the walls of a building, either square or polygonal in plan.

bead

in glazing, an applied sealant in a joint irrespective of the method of application, such as caulking bead, glazing bead, etc. Also a molding or stop used to hold glass or panels in position.

bead and reel

a decorative motif consisting of oval motifs alternating with round or elongated bead-shaped motifs. Much used in the ancient world and copied in the Middle Ages.

beak-head

an ornamental motif resembling a bird's head with a prominent beak. It was common in English

Romanesque architectural decoration.

■ **beam**

1. a horizontal supporting member of a structural frame used to strengthen floors, ceilings, and roofs; usually tied in to the outer structure.
2. structural support member (steel, concrete, lumber) transversely supporting a load that transfers weight from one location to another
3. structural member, other than a triangulated frame, which supports load primarily by its internal resistance to bending.

■ **bearer**

a sub floor timber beam placed across piers or stringers and supporting floor joists.

■ **bearing partition**

a partition that supports any vertical load in addition to its own weight.

■ **bearing wall**

a wall that supports any vertical load in addition to its own weight.

■ **beaux-arts**

a late 19th Century, early 20th Century architectural school that believed in using grandiose styles. Structures are usually symmetrical, using revival elements from Italian Renaissance, Greek Revival, Classical Revival and other ornate styles. Many times these styles were mixed, creating an eclectic work. The style was primarily used for public buildings such as courthouses, libraries, museums and mansions.

■ **bed molding**

a molding in an angle, as between the over hanging cornice, or eaves, of a building and the side walls.

■ **bed or bedding**

in glazing, the bead compound or sealant applied between a light of glass or panel and the stationary stop or sight bar of the sash or frame. It is usually the first bead of compound or sealant to be applied when setting glass or panels.

■ **beed and reel**

a molding. A thin line of decorative molding alternating between sets of beadlike elements and cylindrical elements.

■ **bell reducer**

in plumbing, a fitting shaped like a bell, which has one opening of a smaller diameter used to reduce the size of the pipe in the line, and the opposite opening of larger diameter.

■ **bellcast**

an eave or roof that flares out and is bell-shaped

■ below grade

the portion of a building that is below ground level.

■ belt course

decorative horizontal band on building, usually composed of projecting and/or contrasting stone or brick

■ belvedere

1. a raised turret or pavillion.
2. open sided structure designed to offer extensive views, normally in a formal garden.

■ bending moment

a system of internal forces whose resultant is a moment. This term is most commonly used to refer to internal forces in beams.

■ bent glass

flat glass that has been shaped while hot into curved shapes.

■ berm

1. flat space between the base of the curtain wall and the inner edge of the moat; level area separating ditch from bank.
2. An artificial ridge of earth.

■ bevel

1. any angle not at 90 degrees. Also, a tool for marking such an angle.
2. the angle of the front edge of a door usually from 1/8' to 2'.

■ bevel siding (or lap siding)

wedge-shaped boards used as horizontal siding in a lapped pattern. This siding varies in butt thickness from ½ to ¾ inch and in widths up to 12 inches. Normally used over some type of sheathing.

■ bid bond

security posted by a bidder to ensure performance in accordance with a bid.

■ bid documents

drawings, details, and specifications for a particular project.

■ bidding

getting prices from various contractors and/or subcontractors.

■ billet molding

a molding composed wholly or in part of a series of billets small cubes, cylinders or prisms placed at regular intervals, so that their axis and that of the entire series is parallel to the general direction of the molding.

■ biodeterioration

the breaking down of timber by natural or biological agents such as fungi and insects.

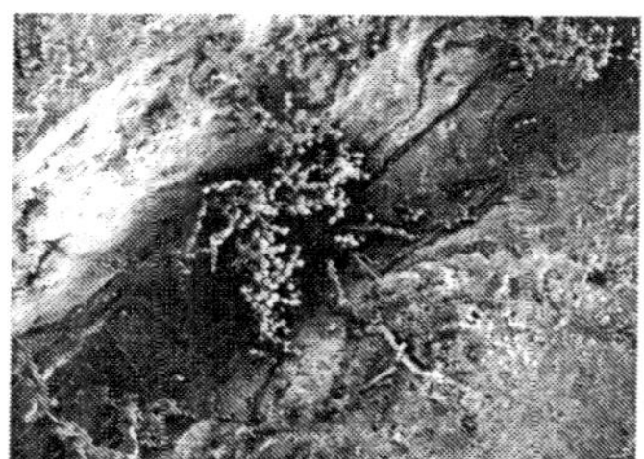

bipedales

Roman bricks measuring two roman feet a side.

birds eye

figure on the surface of wood that has numerous rounded areas resembling small eyes.

bird's-mouth

the notch in a rafter that rests on the top plate of a wall.

bisellia

Latin: seat of honour, seat for two persons. A stone or marble structure built in the form of a canopy; ornamented canopy supported by columns or suspended from a roof or projected from a wall; a covering (usually of cloth) that serves as a roof to shelter an area from the weather; example as seen in the Greco-Roman theatre at Miletus, Turkey; seat of honour in the Roman theatre; seat of honour awarded for municipal services in province

bite

the dimension by which the framing system overlaps the edge of the glazing infill.

bitumen

any of various mixtures of hydrocarbons occurring naturally or obtained through the distillation of coal or petroleum.

bivalate

a hillfort defended by two concentric ditches.

black water

waste water generated by toilets, kitchen sinks, and dishwashers.

bleeding

a migration of a liquid to the surface of a component or into/onto an adjacent material.

blind arcade

a row of decorative arches applied to a wall.

blind arch

an arch applied to a wall. Compare with blind arcade, relieving arch block, cushion, or cubic capital A simple cube-like capital with bottom corners tapered. The block capital is particularly characteristic of Ottomanian and Romanesque architecture in Germany and England. See **capital, column.**

blind nailing

nailing in such a way that the nail heads are not visible on the face of the work—usually at the tongue of matched boards.

blind stop

a rectangular moulding, usually ¾ by 1-3/8 inches or more in width, used in the assembly of a window frame. Serves as a stop for storm and screen or combination windows and to resist air infiltration.

blister

an enclosed raised spot evident on the surface of a building. They are mainly caused by the expansion of trapped air, water vapour, moisture or other gases.

blockhouse

small square fortification, usually of timber bond overlapping arrangement of bricks in courses (Flemish, Dutch, French, etc.)

blocking

in carpentry, the process of fastening together two pieces of board by gluing blocks of wood in the interior angle.

blue prints

architectural plans for a building or construction project, which are likely to include floor plans, footing and foundation plans, elevations, plot plans, and various schedules and or details.

blue stain

a bluish or greyish discoloration of the sapwood caused the growth of certain mold like fungi on the surface and in the interior of a piece, made possible by the same conditions that favour the growth of other fungi.

board

1. a piece of sawn, hewn, or dressed timber of greater width than thickness. Usually 19 mm to 38 mm thick and 75 mm or more wide.
2. Manufactured products supplied as rigid or semi-rigid sheets, e.g. fibreboard and particle boards.

board and batten siding

wall construction for a timber-frame (building) in which the exterior covering consists of closely spaced boards set vertically, with narrow wood strip covering the joints between the boards.

board foot

in carpentry, the equivalent of a board 1 foot square and 1 inch thick.

boards

yard lumber less than 2 inches thick and 2 or more inches wide.

bodied linseed oil

1. linseed oil that has been thickened in viscosity by suitable processing with heat or chemicals. Bodied oils are obtainable in a great range in viscosity from a little greater than that of raw oil to just short of a jellied condition.
2. Linseed oil in which enough lead, manganese or cobalt salts have been incorporated to make the oil harden more rapidly when spread in thin coatings.

body force

an external force acting throughout the mass of a body. Gravity is a body force. An inertial force is a body force.

bolster

a short horizontal timber or steel beam on top of a column to support and decrease the span of beams or girders.

bond

an arrangement of bricks in courses.

bond breaker

a substance or a tape applied between two adjoining materials to prevent adhesion between them.

bond plaster

in addition to gypsum, bond plaster contains 2-5% lime by weight and chemical additives, which improve the bond with dense nonporous surfaces such as concrete. It is used as a base coat.

bonnet

freestanding fortification; priest's cap.

boomtown architecture

style of architecture characteristic of frontier towns that were built quickly. A typical feature is the false front which conceals a more modest structure

boss

1. central stone of arch or vault; key stone.
2. a projecting stone at the intersection of the ribs of a vault, often the keystone and frequently carved.
3. projection, usually carved, at the intersection of stone ribs of Gothic vaults and ceilings.
4. in a vault, large carved pieces used to hide the intersection of the ribs.

boston ridge

a method of applying asphalt or wood shingles at the ridge or at the hips of a roof as a finish.

bouleterion

1. the name of this ancient Greek building type comes from 'boule', the council of the 'polis'. It was used to hold public meetings, the council chamber. It was roofed and had tiers of benches on three sides either rectangular or semicircular in shape. The columns that were used to support the roof interrupted the view of some of the attendees.
2. building for members of the council chamber; an assembly hall for magistrates; town hall

bound moisture

moisture which is closely bound to the cell wall constituents of wood.

bound water

water molecules bound into the cell wall of timber. They are weakly bound chemically to the molecules of the cell wall and energy is required to break them free.

bow

1. a curve, bend, warping or other deviation from flatness in glass or wood.
2. a curvature in the longitudinal direction of a board causing the wide face to move away from a flat plane.

■ bow window

these windows project out from the front or side of a house. Bow windows are rounded. They are often formed of the window glass itself and do not have any structure beneath it. These windows may be found on any level of a building.

■ bowstring truss

a truss where the top chord of the truss is curved to an arch shape.

■ box beam

a built-up beam with solid timber flanges and plywood or wood-base panel product webs.

■ brace

an inclined piece of framing lumber applied to wall or floor to stifled the structure. Often used on walls as temporary bracing until framing has been completed.

■ bracing

1. secondary structural members that normally do not support gravity loads but are required to provide lateral stability to other structural members or to transfer horizontal loads to the supports.
2. ties and rods used for supporting and strengthening various parts of a building used for lateral stability for columns and beams.

■ bracket

1. ornamental support for roof cornice, or arch or entablature.
2. a projecting support for a balcony or roof, sometimes decorated with scrolls or volutes.
3. either a supportive or decorative member used under eaves, stairs, or other locations, which need addition assistance to carry load.

■ brake metal

sheet metal that has been bent to the desired configuration.

■ bratice

a timber tower, or projecting wooden gallery.

■ breastplate/cuirass

body armour, usually made of bronze, worn by Greek soldiers to protect their back and chest. It was the main piece of body armour protecting all upper organs. Cuirasses were made to measure each man being specially fitted. The more expensive cuirasses would have ridges, roughly aligned to the body muscles, which were meant to deflect blows.

■ **breastwork**

heavy parapet slung between two gate towers; defence work over the portcullis.

■ **bressumer**

beam to support a projection.

■ **brick veneer**

a facing of brick laid against and fastened to sheathing of a frame wall or tile wall construction.

■ **bridging**

1. bracing installed between floor joists to stiffen floor and distribute live loads. Also called cross bridging.
2. small wood or metal members that are inserted in a diagonal position between the floor joists at midspan to act both as tension and compression members for the purpose of bracing the joists a spreading the action of loads.

■ **brittle**

a brittle structure or material exhibits low ductility, meaning that it exhibits very little inelastic deformation before complete failure.

■ **broach spire**

octagonal spire rising from a square tower without a parapet, with pyramidal forms at the angles.

■ **broch**

drystone freestanding tower with interior court, no external windows (which face into the court), spiral stair inside wall, typically iron age Celtic refuge in Scotland.

■ **bronze**

a metal made up of a mixture of copper and tin.

■ **bronze age**

from 3000 - 1800 BCE there were three great civilisations, the Cycladic, Minoan, and Mycenaean civilisations, that were inspired by the introduction of bronze working in Greece.

■ **browncoat**

the coat of plaster directly beneath the finish coat. In three-coat work, the brown is the second coat.

■ **bubbling**

in glazing, open or closed pockets in a sealant caused by release, production or expansion of gasses.

■ **buck**

often used in reference to rough frame opening members. Door bucks used in reference to metal door frame.

■ **bucrania**

decorative reliefs of the skulls or heads of cattle or oxen. At times linked by swags of vegetal motifs such as on the Ara Pacis.

building brick

brick for building purposes not especially treated for texture or colour, formerly called 'common brick.' It is stronger than face brick.

building material ecological sustainability index

the building material ecological sustainability index is based on life cycle assessment but attempts to combine a number of criteria into three primary ones. There are:

- resource depletion
- inherent pollution &
- embodied energy.

These characteristics within these criteria are given a rating from 1 (not important) to 5 (very important) in terms of their environmental impact.

building paper

a general term for papers, felts, and similar sheet materials used in buildings without reference to their properties or uses.

building permit

written authorisation from the city, county or other governing regulatory body giving permission to construct or renovate a building. A building permit is specific to the building project described in the application.

building type

in architecture, 'type' can describe function or form. For the purposes of this course, we will use type to describe function. For example, an ancient Greek temple is a structure built to protect the god statue and serve as a focus of religious practice. 'Temple' is the building type, whereas the name of the large temple in the sacred precinct at Athens is the 'Parthenon' (Temple dedicated to Athena Parthenos.) The advantage to this method, or classification system, is that functional types are indicative of societal values. For example, if a society has numerous and varied examples of structures for religious purposes (monastery, church, cathedral, chapel), one could understand the importance of religion to that society.
2. a structure, component, or space that exists or has existed at some time in the past.

built-up roof

a roofing composed of three to five layers of asphalt felt laminated with coal tar, pitch, or asphalt. The top is finished with crushed slag or gravel. Generally used on flat or low-pitched roofs.

bullfloat

a tool used to finish and flatten a slab. Sometimes substituted for darbying. A large flat or tool usually of wood, aluminium or magnesium with a handle.

burg

German stronghold.

burh

Saxon stronghold; literally a 'neighbourhood'.

■ burl

a hard, woody outgrowth on a tree, more or less rounded in form, usually resulting from the entwined growth of a cluster of buds. Such burls are the source of the highly figured burl veneers used for purely ornamental purposes. In lumber or veneer, a localised severe distortion of the grain generally rounded in outline.

■ buttress

1. a supporting section of stonework, mostly outside, perpendicular to a wall.
2. a projecting support built into or against the external wall of a building, typically used in Gothic buildings.
3. an exterior masonry structure that opposes the lateral thrust of an arch or a vault and adds extra support.
4. an exterior mass of masonry set at an angle to or bonded into a wall which it strengthens or supports; buttresses often absorb lateral thrusts from roof vaults.

■ butt glazing

the installation of glass products where the vertical glass edges are without structural supporting mullions.

■ butt joint

1. the junction where the ends of two timbers or other members meet in a square-cut joint.
2. an end joint formed by abutting the squared ends of two pieces.

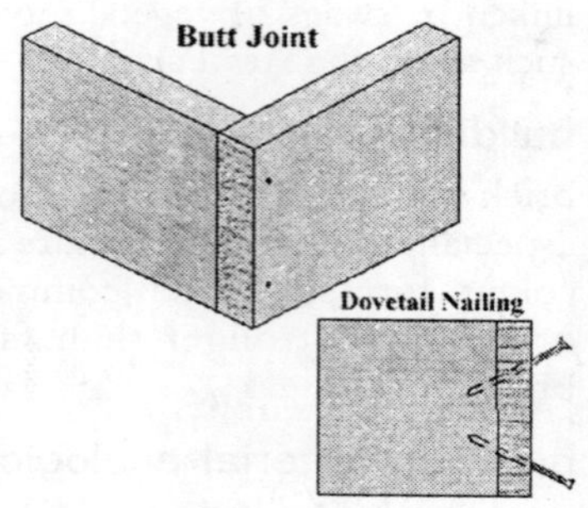

■ butterfly roof

a roof assembly, which pitches sharply from either side toward the centre.

■ buttering

in glazing, application of sealant or compound to the flat surface of some member before placing the member in position, such as the buttering of a removable stop before fastening the stop in place.

■ buttery

next to the kitchen, a room from where wine was dispensed.

■ butyl

type of non-curing and non-skinning sealant made from butylene. Usually used for internal applications.

■ BX armoured cable

a factory assembly of insulated conductors inside a flexible metallic covering. It can be run except where exposed to excessive moisture and should not be run below grade. It must always be grounded and uses its armour as an equipment ground. It is difficult to pull out old wires or insert new ones.

■ Byzantine

a style dating from the fifth century, characterised by masonry construction around a central plan, with domes on penditives, typically depicting the figure of Christ; foliage patterns on stone capitals; and interiors decorated with mosaics and frescos.

■ Byzantine period

the Roman Emperor Constantine I moved the capital of the Roman Empire to present day Istanbul in 324 A.D. and it formally became the Byzantine Empire at the end of the 4th century when Rome went into decline. There were invasions of Goths, Visigoths, Vandals, Ostrogoths, Bulgars, Huns, and Salvs in this period, but Christianity, blended with Hellenism, had taken a strong hold. Christianity was declared the official religion in Greece in 394 A.D. and Greek and Roman gods were branded as pagan and outlawed. Even classical philosophy was forbade in 529 A.D. and replaced with Christian theology. The Byzantine Empire lasted until the fall of Constantinople to the Crusaders in 1205 A.D. and the Ottomans in 1453 A.D.

■ caique

a small, wooden fishing boat often used to transport people to beaches on the Greek islands.

■ calcium chloride

a chemical used to speed up curing of concrete during damp conditions.

■ caldarium

the hot bath and 'sauna' of a Roman bath complex.

■ camber

intentional vertical curve built into a beam or truss to offset load deflection or to improve its appearance.

■ campanile

1. a bell tower usually not actually attached to a church; also, lofty towers that form parts of buildings.
2. Italian name for a bell tower, usually one that is detached from the main building.
3. campanile is the Italian word for bell tower.

■ canon tables

a table of concordance for two or more parallel texts of the Gospels, usually the one compiled by Eusebius of Caesarea in the fourth century.

■ canopy

an overhanging roof.

■ cant strip

a beveled support used at the junction of a flat surface and a vertical surface to prevent bends and/or cracking of the roofing membrane at the intersection of the roof deck and wall. Used with a base flashing to minimise breaking of the roofing felts.

■ cantilever

1. a horizontal projection, such as a balcony or beam, supported at one end only.
2. a projecting structural member which is rigidly fixed at one end but unsupported at the other.

■ cap

the upper member of a column, pilaster, door cornice, molding, and the like.

■ cap sheets

in roofing, one to four plies of felt bonded and top coated with bitumen that is laid over an existing roof as a treatment for defective roofs.

■ cape chisel

tool used to clean out mortar joints on brick.

■ capital

1. distinctly treated upper end of a column.
2. decorative element that divides a column or pier from the masonry which it supports. See **column, pier, shaft, base, abacus.**
3. crowning feature of a column, usually carved.
4. the top section of an architectural column.
5. the top portion of a column or pilaster. The middle section is called the shaft of the column and the bottom, the base.
6. the topmost element of the column, helps to transfer loads from beams to columns. In classical Greek architecture, there are three formal types: the Doric, Ionic and Corinthian. The Corinthian was rarely used by the Greeks, as it was considered too 'showy', but it was very popular with the Romans.

■ carbide bit

tool used to drill holes in brick or block.

■ carbon sink

a carbon sink is something that removes or stores carbon dioxide from the atmosphere, for example growing vegetation.

■ carolingian

the title of this period owes its origin to Charles Martel, the Frankish ruler who defeated the Moors at Poitiers in 732. The artistic advances of this period were initiated by Martel's grandson Charlemagne, who was crowned Holy Roman Emperor in 800. Although the Carolingian empire itself would not survive past the ninth century, the civilising forces set in motion during this era would form the foundation for cultural growth during the Medieval age. Rare examples of Carolingian architecture remain, excepting such sites as Minster at Aachen.

■ carotid

heart-shaped.

■ carpenter gothic

a building style commonly used in homes and churches that is simple, but makes use of Gothic elements such as pointed (lancet) windows with tracery and decorative woodwork such as 'gingerbread'. The name comes from the fact that these buildings were almost always designed and built by a local carpenter or builder.

■ caryatid

1. sculptured female figure serving as a supporting column.
2. Carved female figure used as a supporting column in classical architecture.

■ case hardening

1. a drying defect characterised by the presence of compression stresses in the outer zone and tensile stresses in the core. It occurs when rapid drying has caused permanent set of the outer zones of a piece of wood.
2. when stone is first taken from the ground, it is relatively soft. As it dries out, and salts are drawn to the surface, a patina or harder outer skin known as the case hardening, is formed.

■ casein glue

an adhesive, primarily for internal use, prepared from casein, sodium silicate, lime, soda and other compounds. It was used largely in plywood manufacturer, has some resistance to water but is not waterproof, ages well and can be made resistant to mould.

■ casemates

artillery emplacements in separate protected rooms, rather than in a battery.

■ casement frames and sash

frames of wood or metal enclosing part or all of the sash, which may be opened by means of hinges affixed to the vertical edges.

■ casement windows

a window that hinges or pivots like a door.

■ casing

molding of various widths and thicknesses used to trim door and window openings at the jambs.

cast concrete

concrete that is placed in its mold at the location where it will be used in a building and then allowed to harden (cure) before the mold is removed.

castellan

the officer in charge of a castle.

castrum

1. fortress for any military purpose.
2. the Imperial Roman military camp, an extremely rigid and orderly square, divided into four quadrants by the primary roads and oriented to the cardinal directions. This form, which was originally used for the temporary camps of the soldiers in new colonies, became the built form of those cities.

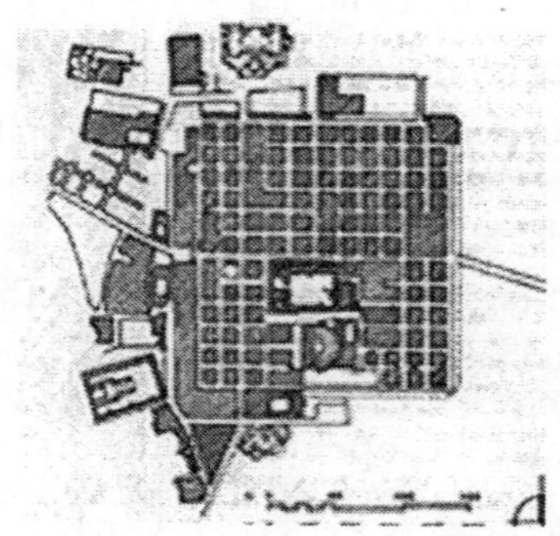

catacomb

1. subterranean burial chamber used during the Roman Empire. Catacombs were used for burial, not only by Christians, but they are usually associated with Christianity because the Christians held services in the catacombs while they were still persecuted by the Romans (First to early fourth centuries A.D., though the persecution was not always severe at all times during this period). Some of the catacombs are decorated with Christian paintings. Compare with crypt. See **sarcophagus, mausoleum.**
2. a verbal surrogate for a group of items or for an individual architectural drawing or other architectural document. A catalogue entry consists of information recorded in a number of categories. See **category of information. of information**
3. a distinct piece of information that pertains to an entity, such as a group, item, subject, built work, person, corporate body, or geographic location.

cathedra

1. the chair on which the bishop sits. It is located in the chancel, often cantered behind the high altar.
2. the Bishop's chair, found in the choir.

cathedral

1. the term cathedral refers to the function of a church, not its architectural style. A cathedral is a church that serves as a bishop's headquarters, so to speak. It's called a cathedral because it contains his cathedra.
2. a Bishop's church, from cathedra, the bishop's chair, positioned behind the altar, in the centre of the apse.
3. the church containing the catherda, the church at the head of a diocese where the Bishop of that diocese sits.

cathedral cut

a variation of the crown cut method of slicing veneers. The growth rings are exactly parallel to the slicer, producing on the face of the veneer an inverted 'V' figure resembling the spire of a cathedral.

caulk

the application of sealant to a joint, crack or crevice. A compound used for sealing that has minimum joint movement capability; sometimes called low performance sealant.

cavea

Latin: also cavea - hollow place, cavity, auditorium/theatre or seats/audience; the audience seating portion of the Roman theatre auditorium.

CCA

Copper Chrome Arsenate, a wood preservative

cella

the interior chamber of an ancient temple between the sidewalls; the sanctuary. It is the main part of the temple where the worshipped statue was erected and is separate from the open Porticoes.

cement types

type I Normal is a general purpose cement suitable for practically all uses in residential construction but should not be used where it will be in contact with high sulphate soils or be subject to excessive temperatures during curing.

type II Moderate is used where precaution against moderate sulphate attack is important, as in drainage structures where sulphate concentrations in groundwater is higher than normal.

type III High Early Strength is used when high strengths are desired at very early periods, usually a week or less. It is used when it is desirable to remove forms as soon as possible or to put the concrete into service quickly.

type IV Low Heat is a special cement for use where the amount and rate of heat generated during curing must be kept to a minimum. The development of strength is slow and is intended in large masses of concrete such as dams.

type V Sulphate Resisting is a special cement intended for use only in construction exposed to severe sulphate action, such as western states having soils of high alkali content.

cenotaph

a monument or building which is an empty tomb, i.e., the person commemorated is buried elsewhere.

■ **centaurs**

mythological wild creatures that were half man half horse. They lived in the Mountains of Pelion and Orsa of Thessaly.

■ **centre of gravity**

the location of the resultant of gravity forces on an object or objects sometimes called centre of mass.

■ **centrally-planned building**

a building in which the sides are of equal length and in which the main space is symmetrical when bisected laterally and longitudinally. A centrally planned building may be square, circular, or polygonal. The most important feature of a centrally planned building is the open space at the centre of the building, developed around a vertical axis. Contrast with longitudinally-planned building

■ **centroid**

similar to the concept of centre of gravity, except that it applies to a two-dimensional shape rather than an object. For a given shape, the centroid location corresponds to the centre of gravity for a thin flat plate of that shape, made from a homogeneous material.

■ **certificate of occupancy**

a document stating that a building is approved for occupancy. The building authority issues the Certificate of Occupancy.

■ **certification**

forest certification refers to the assessment of forest management by an independent third party auditor according to performance criteria for sustainable wood production.

■ **cesspit**

the opening in a wall in which the waste from one or more garderobes was collected.

■ **CFM (Cubic Feet per Minute)**

the measure of volume of air. When testing systems, find the CFM by multiplying the face velocity times the free area in square feet. The face velocity is the amount of air passing through the face of an outlet or return. Free area is the total area of the openings in the outlet or inlet through which air can pass.

■ **chain of custody**

the process by which the source of a timber product is verified. This entails 'tracking' the timber from the forest through all the steps of the production process until it reaches the end user. The process is usually necessary before a timber product can be labelled as being produced from a sustainable source.

■ **chair rail**

a moulding that runs horizontally along the wall at about 3 feet from the ground. In storefront, window wall, or curtain wall systems, a chair rail is an aluminium extrusion applied horizontally to the inside of the system 3 feet from the floor to create a barrier in floor-to-ceiling glazing applications.

■ **chalice**

a cup on a stem, used to contain the ecuharistic wine; the same shape was also used in a secular context See **paten, pyx.**

■ **chamfer**

surface made by smoothing off the angle between two stone faces.

■ **chancel**

in churches with a historic floor plan, the chancel is the front part of the church from which the service is conducted, as distinct from the nave, where the congregation sits. The chancel is usually an elevated platform; usually three steps up from the nave. In churches with a lecture-hall floor plan, the term sanctuary is often used to mean both chancel and nave because the two are not architecturally distinct. In the historic floor plan, the words chancel and sanctuary are often synonyms.

■ **chancel arch**

the arch, which separates the chancel (sanctuary or choir) from the nave of a church. See **nave, choir.**

■ **chancel/chancel arch**

the continuation of the nave, east of the crossing, where the altar is placed. The chancel arch occurs where the chancel meets the crossing.

■ **channel glazing**

the installation of glass products into U-shaped glazing channels. The channels may have fixed stops; however, at least one glazing stop on one edge must be removable.

■ **chantry chapel**

a chapel paid for by a rich family of the area. Often contains tombs of said family.

■ **chapel**

1. a chapel can either be an alcove with an altar in a large church, or a separate building that is smaller than a full-sized church. Chapels have the same function as church buildings and are equipped the same way, but they are usually dedicated to special use. For example, a large estate might have a chapel in which worship services are held for family members, staff, and guests. If a church builds a new and larger sanctuary, but keeps the old one, the old one is often called a chapel.
2. most popularly applies to a private place of worship, but can be part of a church, where often, worship of a particular saint is implied.

■ **chapter house**

1. a meeting place for the chapter or governing body of a monastery or a cathedral. Other parts of monastery cloister, refectory, scriptorium.
2. room in which the chapter (the governing body of the diocese) meets. Often circular or polygonal, with carving and large windows.

■ **check**

a separation of fibres along the grain forming a fissure, but not extending through the piece from face to face. Checks commonly resulting from stresses built up during seasoning. They run radially, across the growth rings.

■ **checking**

fissures that appear with age in many exterior paint coatings, at first superficial, but which in time may penetrate entirely through the coating. It produces a pattern of surface cracks running in irregular lines. When found in the top pour of an asphalt built-up roof, checking is the preliminary stage of alligatoring.

■ **checkrails**

meeting rails sufficiently thicker than a window to fill the opening between the top and bottom sash made by the parting stop in the frame of double-hung windows. They are usually beveled.

■ **chemical injection grouting**

leak repair technique usually used below grade in cracks and joints in concrete walls and floors that involves injection of sealant (usually urethane) that reacts with water to form a seal.

■ **chemise wall**

formed by a series of interlinked or overlapping semicircular bastions.

■ **chevet**

1. the eastern end of a Gothic church, including choir (quire), ambulatory, and radiating chapels.
2. French term for the east end of the church when composed of an apse, ambulary and radiating chapels, as found in Westminster Abbey.

■ **chevron**

a zig-zag motif. See **other repetitive decorative motifs (twelfth century).**

■ **chisel**

a wedge-like, sharp-edged tool used for cutting or shaping timber.

■ **chiton**

1. basic item of clothing for both man and women in ancient Greece. Chitons were made from two rectangles of fabric fastened at the shoulders and down the sides and tied at the waist.
2. basic garment of ancient Greece, worn knee-length by men and full-length by women.

■ **choir**

1. the part of a cruciform church east of the crossing.
2. the area of the church between a transept and main apse. It is the area where the service is sung and clergy may stand, and the main or high altar is located. In some churches there is no choir, while in others, the choir is quite large and surrounded by an ambulatory. See **altar, choir screen.**
3. where divine service is sung, usually part of the chancel.
4. properly, the area of the church from where services are sung, sometimes this term refers to the eastern arm of a cruciform church.
5. the space reserved for the clergy in the church, usually east

of the transept but, in some instances, extending into the nave.

choir screen

a screen, made of wood or stone, usually decorated with painting or sculpture, which separates the choir from the rest of the church. See **choir.**

chord

either of the two outside members of a truss (a) connected and braced by the web (b) members. The term also applies to beam flanges or the perimeter members of a plywood diaphragm.

church design

a church is a building set aside for public worship, Christianity is implied. The recognised form of Christian architecture evolved from the early 4th century. The religious circle has survived, but the most usual plan form is the cross, the Latin cross where one arm is longer than the others prevailed. Verticality was sought for both symbolic and practical reasons, spires were added to towers to form steeples, and internally, an impression of height was achieved with the nave, chancel and transepts, lit from clerestory windows high in the walls where they avoided the roofs of the aisles. The longest part of the church is traditionally orientated east/west, with the altar at the eastern end. The main entrance is usually at the west end. Not all churches followed this design of course, the more austere were happy to worship in 'God Boxes' plain rectangles, sometimes with a spire.

ciborium

1. a box in which the Host (wafers or bread for the Eucharist) is kept, compare pxy.
2. A canopy resting on columns over the altar. See **paten, chalice**

cinqfoil

a five-lobed ornamental shape. Compare with trefoil, quatrefoil

cinquefoil

a five-lobed carved circle or arch head.

circuit breaker

simple switch-like device, which automatically opens a circuit when the rated current is exceeded as in the case of a short circuit.

circus

in ancient Roman architecture, the structure built for the running and viewing of chariot races. The Circus Maximus, or Domition's Circus, in Rome seated 200,000 people. The space of this circus survives today as the Piazza Navona.

■ city-state

a conventional city that with its surrounding territory, is also an independent political state. Ancient Greece was made up of a number of independent city states like Athens, Corinth, Sparta ... and more.

■ cladding

the external covering or skin of walls of a building. Timber cladding includes natural or treated timber boards, and plywood.

■ clapboard

1. long, thin, overlapping, horizontal wooden boards used on the exterior of framed construction as a waterproof exterior covering.
2. siding use to clad the exterior of a building. Clapboards are installed by slightly overlapping boards that have one edge wider than another.

■ clasping

encasing the angle.

■ classical architecture

classical denotes superiority. Classicus was a title reserved for a superior member of Roman society. First applied to literature, the use of the term was expanded, to include the architecture of ancient Greece and Rome. It's origins lie in the way the Greeks constructed their first temples. The constructional elements of these first timber buildings were developed and adapted to stone construction. Respect for tradition saw the preservation of many of the timber details, used as decorative elements. A complex code evolved based on columns and beams which used an exact proportional system to correct the optical distortion, which can result in buildings appearing to splay outwards or curve downwards. Special combinations of columns, base, shaft and capital, and the entablature above, evolved to be known as orders. Invented by the Greeks, and used and adapted by the Romans, they were revived in the Renaissance. The earliest was the Doric (Dorian tribes) followed by the Ionic (Ionians) and the Corin-thian. The Romans added two more, the Tuscan (Etruscans) and the Composite orders. Each order has its own peculiar decoration and proportional relationship between its various parts. The size of buildings may vary, but these proportional relationships stay constant. Eventually the orders became personalised, with the sturdy Doric and Tuscan seen as representing the masculine figure, the more slender Ionic the older woman, the matron, and the graceful Corinthian and Composite, the younger woman, the maiden. The Romans continued to build in the tradition of the Greeks, devising their own orders, but their needs were different, they made use of the arch and where the Greeks seldom used mortar, the Romans developed cements and concretes which allowed them to fully exploit rounded forms. They often built to four and five storeys, as opposed to the Greeks two, and the orders steadily became more decorative than functional.

classical period

from 480 - 338 BCE, the Classical Period is marked by the rise in and affluence of Athens, the Peloponnesian Wars, the falls of Athens, and the eventual decline of all of the city-states from years of fighting.

classical revival

1. the Italian Renaissance or neoclassical movements in England and the United States in the nineteenth century that looked to the traditions of Greek and Roman antiquity.
2. also frequently referred to as Neoclassical Revival. Ancient Roman and Greek architecture inspired architecture. The style can be described as monumental, utilising columns, pediments and sparing ornamentation. The style is most frequently found in public buildings and mansions.

classicism

a tradition of Greek and Roman antiquity, distinguished by the qualities of simplicity, harmony, and balance.

clathri window (lattice window)

windows that have wood or metal strips that divide glass in a diagonal pattern to create an ornamental effect.

clear span

the clear horizontal distance between the supports of a load bearing member

cleat

a wedge-shaped piece (usually of metal) which serves as a support or check. A strip fastened across something to give strength or hold something in position.

cleavage test

a test that measures the resistance of a timber to splitting longitudinally along the radial and tangential planes.

clepsydra

Greek or Roman water clock used for timing speakers; time of one clock (20 minutes.)

cloister

1. in religious institutions, a courtyard with covered walks.
2. part of a monastery; a quadrangle surrounded by covered passages. It connects the domestic parts of the monastery with the church. Usually located on the south side of the church. Other parts of monastery chapter house, refectory, scriptorium.
3. a court, usually with covered walks or ambulatories along its sides.

cloister vault or segmented dome

a dome placed over a polygonal base. It is not a semi-sphere, but is formed of curved sections which correspond to the parts of the polygon on which it rests.

Compare with pendentive, squinch.

■ cloisters

an enclosed space, usually on the south side of the nave, connecting the church to the domestic parts of the monastery. Characterised by covered walkways.

■ close- grained wood

1. wood with narrow, inconspicuous growth rings. The term is sometimes used to designate wood having small and closely spaced pores, but in this sense the term 'fine textured' is more often used.
2. wood with wide conspicuous growth rings in which there is considerable difference between early-wood and late-wood. The term is sometimes used to designate wood with large pores, but in this sense the term 'coarse textured' is more often used.

■ clunch

hard chalky material.

■ coach screw

similar to a wood screw except larger and with a hexagonal head so that it can be turned with a spanner.

■ coal tar pitch

a bituminous material, which is a by-product from the coking of coal. It is used as the waterproofing material for tar and gravel built-up roofing.

■ coating

a layer of any liquid product spread over a surface for protection.

■ cob

unburned clay mixed with straw.

■ codex (plural codices)

a manuscript that is sewn together in the form of a book, with a spine and often a cover. The codex form replaced the scroll as the most common form of manuscript in the early Christian period.

■ coffer

1. the sunken area created between the crossing of structural members. Coffers often appear in a flat ceiling or on the interior surface of a dome. They are often the focus of decoration and serve also to lighten the weight of the structure.
2. an inset decoration in a ceiling, vault, or dome. They range from the undecorative types such as in the inner dome of the Pantheon, to more ornate ones decorated with moldings and rosettes.

■ cohesive failure

internal splitting of a compound resulting from over-stressing of the compound.

■ cold applied

products that can be applied without heating. These are in contrast to products which need to be heated to be applied.

■ cold patch

in roofing, a roof repair done with cold-applied material.

■ collapse

the flattening of single cells or rows of cells during the drying or pressure treatment of wood. Often characterised by a caved-in or corrugated ('washboarded') appearance of the wood surface.

■ collar

in roofing, a conical metal cap flashing used in conjunction with vent pipes or stacks usually located several inches above the plane of the roof, for the purpose of shedding water away from the base of the vent.

■ collar beam

in carpentry, a tie that keeps the roof from spreading. They serve to stiffen the roof structure. Connects similar rafters on opposite sides of roof.

■ collar tie

a horizontal board that connects pairs of rafters on opposite roof slopes.

■ colonnade

1. row of pillars or columns.
2. a row of columns, usually equidistant.
3. a row of columns which support horizontal members, called an architrave, rather than arches. Contrast with arcade. See **architrave, column, pier.**
4. line of columns supporting a row of arches, a roof, an upper story or the top part of a wall.

■ column

1. a vertical support; in an order it consists of a shaft and capital, often resting on a base.
2. pillar (circular section).
3. a free standing axially loaded compression member, usually vertical.
4. a cylindrical support, usually structural but often decorative. other parts of a column abacus or impost block, capital, shaft, base Compare with pier, pilaster. See **applied or engaged column, arcade, colonnade.**
5. in classical architecture, a column consists of a base, shaft and a capital. An engaged column projects about half its thickness from a wall.
6. a vertical weight-carrying architectural member, circular in cross section and consisting of a base (sometimes omitted) a shaft, and a capital.
7. a slender, upright structure used in architecture to support an arch, a roof, an upper story or the top part of a wall. Most columns consist of a base, shaft (the main part) and capital (the decorative section at the top.)
8. in architecture: A perpendicular supporting member, circular or rectangular in section, usually consisting of a base, shaft, and capital. In engineering: A vertical structural compression member which supports loads acting in the direction of its longitudinal axis.
9. the preferred term when indicating the vertical member in a trabeated (post and lintel) system whose section is round. 'Pillar' is rarely used as it connotes monumental scale, as in 'the Pillars of Hercules'.

■ column, commemorative column

the freestanding column in ancient Roman architecture has a commemorative function.
The column of Trajan, built by the Roman emperor Trajan, records Trajan's successful military campaigns in which he extended the empire into what is now Hungary and Romania.

■ column/pillar/post

an upright supporting member used to support ceilings and roofs.

■ combination doors or windows

combination doors or windows used over regular openings. They provide winter insulation and summer protection and often have self storing or removable glass and screen inserts. This eliminates the need for handling a different unit each season.

■ commission

to order something to be made, usually for money.

■ compatible

two or more substances, which can be mixed or blended without separating, reacting, or affecting either material adversely.

■ compluvium

the open roof of an atrium in a Roman house. See impluvium, atrium.

■ component

any one part of an assembly associated with construction.

■ component (of a vector)

any vector can be expressed as a collection of vectors whose sum is equal to the original vector. Each vector in this collection is a component of the original vector. It is common to express a vector in terms of components which are parallel to the x and y axes.

■ composite

1. developed by the Romans, the composite is a mixture of the ionic and corinthian orders. Usually ten-and-a-half diameters in height, the order was richly ornate and was mainly used on triumphal arches.
2. a combination of different elements.

composite board

an insulation board, which has two different insulation types laminated together in 2 or 3 layers.

composite capital (order)

an order consisting of a hybrid of Corinthian and Ionic elements, normally with the acanthus motifs of the Corinthian order surmounted by Ionic volutes at the corners.

composite order

a Roman order; its capital combines the Corinthian acanthus leaf decoration with volutes from the Ionic Order.

composite pier

a type of pier that is composed not of a single member but has shafts, half-columns, or pilaster strips attached to it. See **alternation of support, pier.**

compound

a chemical formulation of ingredients used to produce a caulking, elastomeric joint sealant, etc.

compound pier

a pier composed of a group or cluster of members, especially characteristic of Gothic architecture.

compression

a state or condition of being pushed or shortened by a force.

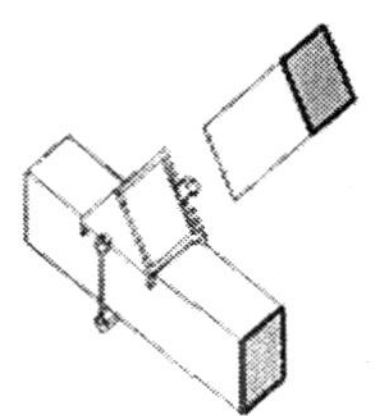

compression failure

deformation or fracture of wood fibres across the grain resulting from excessive compression along the grain.

compression gasket

a gasket designed to function under compression.

compression seat

1. a fabricated or cast metal bracket into which timber structural members abut, used to joint timber compression elements to other structural members.
2. the permanent deformation of a material after removal of the compressive stress.

concentrated force

a force considered to act along a single line in space. Concentrated forces are useful mathematical idealisations, but cannot be found in the real world, where all forces are either body forces acting over a volume or surface forces acting over an area.

concentrated load

an external force which a concentrated force.

concentric

having two sets of walls, one inside the other.

concrete plain

concrete either without reinforcement, or reinforced only for shrinkage or temperature changes.

condensation

the appearance of moisture (water vapour) on the surface of an object caused by warm moist air coming into contact with a colder object. In a building: Beads or drops of water (and frequently frost in extremely cold weather) that accumulate on the inside of the exterior covering of a building when warm, moisture-laden air from the interior reaches a point where the temperature no longer permits the air to sustain the moisture it holds. Use of louvers or attic ventilators will reduce moisture condensation in attics. A vapour barrier under the gypsum lath or dry wall on exposed walls will reduce condensation in them.

■ conditioning treatment

a treatment applied to equilibrate the moisture content of wood to a particular value.

■ conduction

the flow of heat from one part of a substance to another part. A piece of iron with one end placed in a fire will soon become warm from end to end, from the transfer of heat by the actual collision of the air molecules.

■ conductor

in roofing, a pipe for conveying rainwater from the roof gutter to a drain, or from a roof drain to the storm drain; also called a leader, downspout, or down pipe.

■ conduit

a pipe, usually metal, for protecting and routing electrical wiring.

■ confessio

a type of crypt which consists of a series of linked passages. The most famous confessio crypt during the Middle Ages was that of Old Saint Peter's church in Rome, which contained the tomb of Saint Peter. See **crypt.**

■ conglomerate

sedimentary rock construction material composed of large sediments like sand and pebbles cemented together with dissolved minerals such as calcite; building material associated with theatres such as Aspendos or Side; rise of sea-level with consequent flooding of the land are frequently marked by conglomerate deposits

■ connection

connection is similar to the concept of support, except that connection refers to a relationship between members in a structural model. A connection restrains degrees of freedom of one member with respect to another. For each restrained degree of freedom, there is a corresponding force transferred from one member to the other; forces associated with unrestrained degrees of freedom are zero. See **fixed connection.**

■ conservation

the sustainable use of forest resources in a manner that does not degrade the collective resource values of a region over the long term.

■ conservator

someone who is responsible for the care, restoration, and repair of objects.

construction loan

a loan provided by a lending institution specifically to construct or renovate a building.

construction, frame

a type of construction in which the structural parts are wood or depend upon a wood frame for support. In codes, if masonry veneer is applied to the exterior walls, the classification of this type of construction is usually unchanged.

contemporary

a term broadly used to describe architecture constructed between the 1940s through the 1970s. Contemporary buildings frequently have flat roofs, roof decks and broad overhanging eaves. Modern architecture is also a term used as a synonym for Contemporary.

continuity strap

a piece of flat steel fixed over a butt joint between timber beams to provide a continuous tension connection.

contour scaling

the term used to describe the process where salt crystallisation detaches the case hardening.

control joint

1. a vertical or horizontal gap, filled or unfilled, to accommodate differential movement between various elements of a construction.
2. A control joint controls or accommodates movement in the surface component of a roof.

convection

a method of transferring heat by the actual movement of heated molecules, usually by a freestanding unit such as a furnace.

cooling tower

a large device mounted on roofs, consisting of many baffles over which water is pumped in order to reduce its temperature.

coped joint

see **scribing**.

coping

1. covering stones.
2. a construction unit placed at the top of the parapet wall to serve as a cover for the wall.

copper pipe types

type K has the heaviest or thickest wall and is generally used underground. It has a green stripe. Type L has a medium wall thickness and is most commonly used for water service and for general interior water piping. It has a blue stripe. Type M has a thin wall and many codes permit its use in general water piping installation. It has a red stripe.

corbel

1. a projecting block of stone built into a wall during construction; step-wise construction, as in an arch, roof, etc.
2. a projection from a wall which sometimes supports (or appears to support) a structural member such as a shaft.
3. a projecting wall member used as a support for some element of

the superstructure. Also, courses of stone or brick in which each course projects beyond the one beneath it. Two such structures, meeting at the topmost course, creates an arch.
4. a piece of stone projecting from a wall to support a vault of parapet, often decoratively carved.
5. a length of timber laid horizontally on the top of a column to transfer loads and to provide a seat for beams. A compound corbel includes several lengths of timber instead of one.

■ corbel out

to build out one or more courses of brick or stone from the face of a wall, to form a support for timbers.

■ corbelling/corbelled brick

stepped projections of brick or other type of masonry.

■ corbels

brick or masonry that sticks out beyond the one below it to act as a support for a window, chimney stack, or bracket, or that forms an arch or dome.

■ core

1. a small section cut from any material to show internal composition.
2. the basic information necessary to create a minimum catalogue entry.

■ corinthian

1. invented by the Greeks, but not widely used, it was developed by the Romans. The capital has acanthus leaf decoration, which legend bases on a hanging basket. The columns are usually ten diameters in height. The entablature is heavily decorated, with a particularly deep cornice, usually supported on modillions.
2. one of three principal styles (or orders) in classical architecture, Corinthian columns fall between those of the Doric and Ionic orders in diameter and width of fluting and they have elaborate, bell - shaped capitals adorned with acanthus leaves.

■ corinthian architecture

the most ornate of the three orders of classical Greek architecture. The columns have bell-shaped Capitals with adornments based on acanthus leaves.

■ corinthian capital

a capital used originally by the Greeks in a system of supports called the Corinthian order. The Corinthian capital was developed further in Roman times and used often in the medieval period, again, without strict adherence to the rest of the system. It is decorated with 3 superimposed rows of carved foliage (acanthus leaves) around the capital. At the comers of the capital there are small volutes. See **column, capital, abacus or impost block.**

■ corinthian column

1. is a shaft with leaves decorating the capital on top. Click on the term for a review.
2. from the Corinthian order in Classical architecture. The column capital is ornate featuring acanthus

leaves, buds, volutes (scroll shape) and decorative details.

■ corinthian order

1. resembles Ionic in most aspects except for the column capital; Corinthian columns have tall capitals shaped like an upside-down bell and are covered with rows of acanthus leaves and small vine like spirals called helixes; Indeed, the Corinthian order was at first used only for columns inside buildings; did not appear externally until the 4th century BC; use in exterior temple colonnades did not become widespread until Roman times.
2. the last of the three Greek orders, similar to the Ionic, but with the capital decorated with carvings of the acanthus leaf.

■ corner bead

a strip of formed sheet metal, sometimes combined with a strip of metal lath, placed on corners before plastering to reinforce them. Also, a strip of wood finish three-quarters-round or angular placed over a plastered corner for protection.

■ corner boards

used as trim for the external corners of a house or other frame structure against which the ends of the siding are finished.

■ corner braces

diagonal braces at the corners of frame structure to stiffen and strengthen the wall.

■ corner stone

a stone laid in a prominent corner that is engraved with the construction date and other information about the building.

■ cornerite

metal-mesh lath cut into strips and bent to a right angle. Used in interior corners of walls and ceilings on lath to prevent cracks in plastering.

■ cornice

1. the upper part of an entablature, extending beyond the frieze.
2. decorative projection along the top of a wall.
3. projecting upper part of the entablature in classical architecture.
4. the part of a building's entablature or roof element, which projects away from the vertical of the wall.
5. a horizontal projecting course on the exterior of a building, usually at the base of the parapet. In residential construction, the overhang of a pitched roof at the cave line, usually consisting of a facie board, a soffit for a closed cornice, and appropriate mouldings.
6. the exterior trim of a building at the roofline, or a decorative projection from a building, or the top most part of an entablature.

■ cornice return

that portion of the cornice that returns on the gable end of a house.

■ corrosion

the deterioration of metal by chemical or electrochemical reaction resulting from exposure to weathering, moisture, chemicals or other agents or media.

■ **corrugated**

folded or shaped into parallel ridges or furrows so as to form a symmetrically wavy surface.

■ **corrugated metal siding**

rolled metal in parallel ridges and used as siding. Generally made of galvanised steel or aluminium.

■ **corybant**

a follower of Cybele.

■ **cost breakdown**

a breakdowns of all the anticipated costs on a construction or renovation project.

■ **counter flashing**

the formed metal secured to a wall, curb, or roof top unit to cover and protect the upper edge of a base flashing and its associated fasteners. This type of flashing is usually used in residential construction on chimneys at the roofline to cover shingle flashing and to prevent moisture entry.

■ **counterguard**

a long, near-triangular freestanding fortification within the moat.

■ **counterscarp**

the outer slope of a ditch.

■ **coupe**

a defined area of forest, usually with consistent characteristics.

■ **couple**

a system of forces composed of two equal forces of opposite direction, offset by a distance. A couple is statically equivalent to a moment whose magnitude equals the magnitude of the force times the offset distance.

■ **coupler**

a metal sleeve threaded internally and used to connect threaded rods or bolts.

■ **coupling**

in plumbing, a short collar with only inside threads at each end, for receiving the ends of two pipes which are to be fitted and joined together. A right/left coupling is one used to join 2 gas pipes in limited space.

■ **course**

1. level layer of stones or bricks.
2. masonry laid horizontally with mortar to form a wall.
3. a single layer of brick or stone or other building material.

■ **courtyard**

an outdoor room created by at least three sides of a building or several buildings, generally at the building scale.

■ **cove molding**

a molding with a concave face used as trim or to finish interior corners.

■ **covenants**

rules usually developed by a builder or developer regarding the physical appearance of buildings in a particular geographic area. Typical covenants address building height, appropriate fencing and landscaping, and the type of exterior material (stucco, brick, stone, siding, etc) that may be used.

the style frequently features porches with battered columns, exposed roof rafters projecting under the eaves, gabled front porches and dormers. Building materials included stucco, wood shingles, clapboard, brick and stone. The masonry elements were generally on the first floor. Craftsman building frequently featured casement windows as apposed to single or double hung windows. The Craftsman style is considered a return to a simpler, more natural type of architecture and is a direct opposite to the ornate Victorian Era architecture.

■ crannog

Celtic Scotland timber-built fortified lake village.

■ crawl space

a shallow open area between the floor of a building and the ground, normally enclosed by the foundation wall.

■ crazing

a series of hairline cracks in the surface of weathered materials, having a web-like appearance. Also, hairline cracks in pre-finished metals caused by bending or forming.

■ creasing

þ-shaped mark on a wall, marking the pitch of a former roof.

■ creep

increase in deformation following prolonged loading.

■ crenel

the low segment of the alternating high and low segments of a battlement.

■ crenelated

notched or indented, usually with respect to tops of walls, as in battlements.

■ crenelation

battlements at the top of a tower or wall.

■ crenelation or battlement

a parapet with alternating openings (embrasures) and raised sections (merlons), often used on castle walls and towers for defence purposes.

■ crepidoma

the base on which a classical temple sits.

■ cricket

a small drainage-diverting roof structure of single or double slope placed at the junction of larger surfaces that meet at an angle, such as above a chimney.

■ cripple

a cut in an unseasoned joist, bearer or stud designed to reduce movement in a floor or wall as the structural timber seasons.

■ criteria and indicators

a criterion is a category of conditions or processes by which sustainable forest management may be assessed. A criterion is characterised by a set of related indicators that are monitored periodically to assess change. An indicator is a measure (measurement) of an aspect of the criterion. An indicator can be quantitative or qualitative variable which can be measured or described and which, when observed periodically, demonstrates trends.

■ **crocket**

1. curling leaf-shape.
2. a projecting, foliate ornament of a capital, pinnacle, gable or buttress.

■ **crocket capital**

a simplified adaptation of the Corinthian capital. The crocket capital was commonly used in the Gothic period. See column, capital, abacus or impost block.

■ **crockets**

ornamental carved decorations placed at regular intervals on spires, pinnacles, etc.

■ **cross cut**

to cut across the grain.

■ **cross gabled roof**

a roof that has two intersecting gables at right angles.

■ **cross grain**

an arrangement in which the fibres and other longitudinal elements of a piece of wood deviate from a line parallel with the edges of the piece.

■ **cross section**

a diagram showing a building as if it had been cut at right angles to the ground plan. Compare with ground or floor plan.

■ **cross-and-orb**

modified cross slits to accommodate gunnery.

■ **cross-barrel vault**

the main barrel (tunnel) vault is intersected at right angles with other barrel (tunnel) vaults at regular intervals.

■ **cross-bridging**

diagonal bracing between adjacent floor joists, placed near the centre of the joist span to prevent joists from twisting.

■ **crossing**

1. area of a church where the at nave, choir, and transept intersect. See **crossing tower Other parts of a church ambulatory, apse, choir, east end, nave, transept, west end.**
2. the space in a cruciform church formed by the intersection of the nave and the transept.
3. the central point in the church where the nave, choir and trancepts meet.
4. the area of intersection in a Cruciform church, formed by joining the Nave, Transept & Chancel.

■ **crossing pier**

in the interior of a building, a support that is placed at one of the corners of the crossing. See **crossing, crossing tower pier.**

■ **crossing square**

the area in a church that is formed by the intersection (crossing) of a nave and transept of equal width.

crossing tower

the tower which sometimes occurs above the space at the intersection of the nave, chancel, and transept of a church. See **crossing, crossing pier**.

crosswall

interior dividing wall; structural.

crown

top part of arch. including the keystone.

crown cut

a method of slicing veneers whereby the average inclination of the growth rings to the wider face is tangential or less than 45 degrees. This method is also known as flat cut.

crown molding

molding that finishes the junction between a wall and a roof at the eave.

crownwork

freestanding bastioned fortification in front of main defences.

crozier

a staff carried by a bishop, archbishop, abbot or abbess. It is in the shape of a shepherd's crook, and has symbolic significance connected with the New Testament idea of Christ as shepherd of a flock. The crook and staff of the crozier may be heavily decorated.

cruciform

1. in the shape of a cross.
2. cross-shaped. Most Medieval cathedrals are cruciform, with the main axis pointing West-East.

crude mortar joints

when mortar is not finely tooled between courses of brick or stone.

crypt

1. an underground chamber for relics or tombs. See **catacomb types of crypt confessio, hall crypt cubic, cushion, or block capital.** A very simple cube-like capital with bottom corners tapered. The block capital is particularly characteristic of Ottonian and Romanesque Germany and England.
2. a vaulted space under part of a building, wholly or partly underground; in Medieval churches, normally the portion under an apse or a chevet.

cryptoporticus

usually a slightly sunken arcade or barrel vault creating a long walkway or storage area. Architecturally, they often also function as buttressing for larger, adjacent structures. Often lit by openings piercing the upper part of the vault.

cunei

Latin: wedge-shaped stone or area. Roman: wedge shaped seating sections in the cavea (auditorium); corresponds to Greek 'kerkis'.

cup

a concave curvature across the grain or width of the a piece of timber.

cupola

1. hemispherical armoured roof.
2. a small monitor or dome at the peak of a pitched roof.

cupping
the curvature that occurs in the cross section of a piece of timber i.e. in the end of a board.

curb
a short wall or masonry built above the level of the roof that provides a means of flashing the deck equipment.

curia
a governing body and name of the building which housed it. The Curia was a meeting place for the Senate or the town council of a Roman town.

curing
in concrete application, the process in which mortar and concrete harden. The length of time is dependent upon the type of cement, mix proportion, required strength, size and shape of the concrete section, weather and future exposure conditions. The period may be 3 weeks or longer for lean concrete mixtures used in structures such as dams or it may be only a few days for richer mixes. Favourable curing temperatures range from 50 to 70 degrees F. Design strength is achieved in 28 days.

curing agent
one part of a multi-part sealant which, when added to the base, will cause the base to change its physical state by chemical reaction between the two parts.

curtain
a connecting wall 'hung' between towers of a castle.

curtain wall
1. an exterior wall or a section of that wall between two gates or towers. Some castle had two sets of curtain walls.
2. a connecting wall hung between two towers surrounding the bailey.
3. a thin wall, supported by the structural steel or concrete frame of the building independent of the wall below. Also a metal (most often aluminium) framing system on the face of a building containing vision glass panels and spandrel panels made of glass, aluminium, or other material.

curvilinear
characterised by curving lines, as opposed to rectilinear which has straight lines.

cushion
capital cut from a block by rounding off the lower corners.

cusp
1. curves meeting in a point.
2. a curved, triangular-shaped projection from the inner curve of an arch or circle.
3. in arches or tracery, the points between the lobes of the foils.

cut off
a piece of roofing membrane consisting of one or more narrow plies of felt usually moped in hot to seal the edge of insulation at the end of a day's work.

cutback
in roofing, basic asphalt or tar which has been 'cut back' with

solvents and oils so that the material become fluid.

■ **cut-in brace**

nominal 2-inch-thick members, usually 2 by 4's, cut in between each stud diagonally.

■ **cycladic period**

based in the Cyclades Islands from 3000 - 1100 BCE were a civilisation of accomplished sailors who traded all over the Mediterranean and left behind many carved Parian marble figurines. The period is divided into Early (3000 - 2000 BCE), Middle (2000 - 1500 BCE), and Late (1500 - 1100 BCE) phases.

■ **cyclopean**

drystone masonry, ancient, of huge blocks.

■ **cyma recta**

a molding consisting of double elements, concave above, convex below.

■ **cyma reversa**

a molding opposite of the cyma recta, here concave below, convex above.

■ **dado**

1. lower part of an interior wall, often decorated with arcading.
2. lower part of an interior wall when panelled or painted separately from the main part.
3. a rectangular groove across the width of a board or plank. In interior decoration, a special type of wall treatment.

■ **damper**

valve for controlling airflow. When ordering registers, make sure each supply outlet has a damper so the air flow can be adjusted and turned off. Dampers maybe either manually or automatically operated. Automatic dampers are required for exhaust air ducts.

■ **dampproofing**

a process used on concrete, masonry or stone surfaces to repel water, the main purpose of which is to prevent the coated surface from absorbing rain water while still permitting moisture vapour to escape from the structure. (Moisture vapour readily penetrates coatings of this type.) 'Dampproofing' generally applies to surfaces above grade; 'waterproofing' generally applies to surfaces below grade.

■ **darby**

a flat tool used to smooth concrete flatwork immediately after screeding.

■ **dark age**

the period from 1200 - 800 BCE. is also called the Geometric Period. It is named for the demise in city-states due to the ruling and warring Doric civilisation. They created a system of aristocratic landowners and made pottery decorated with geometric designs that is the source of the alternate name for the period.

■ **daub**

a mud of clay mixture applied over wattle to strengthen and seal it.

■ **dead load**

the constant, design-weight (of the roof) and any permanent fixtures attached above or below.

■ **dead-ground**

close to the wall, where the defenders can't shoot.

■ **decay**

1. the decomposition of wood by fungi.
2. disintegration of wood or other substance through the action of fungi,

■ **deck**

an elevated platform. 'Deck' is also commonly used to refer to the above-ground floors in multi-level parking garage.

■ **deck paint**

an enamel with a high degree of resistance to mechanical wear, designed for use on such surfaces as porch floors.

■ **decking**

timber used in surfacing parts of bridges and other structures subjected to vehicular or pedestrian traffic.

■ **decorated**

second of the Gothic styles in Britain, around 1250-1370, typified by highly-decorated designs and elaborate vaulting. Lichfield is a good example.

■ **deflect**

to bend or deform under weight.

■ **deflection**

1. this word usually carries the same meaning as displacement, although it is sometimes used in place of deformation.
2. the amount of bending movement of any part of a structural member perpendicular to the axis of the member under an applied load.

■ **deformation**

a change in the shape of an object or material.

■ **degrade**

in timber and other forest products, the result of any process that lowers the value of the wood.

■ **degree of freedom**

a displacement quantity which defines the shape and location of an object. In the two dimensional plane, a rigid object has three degrees of freedom two translations and one rotation. In three dimensional space, a rigid object has six degrees of freedom (three translations and three rotations.)

■ **dehumidifier kiln**

a kiln working on the heat pump principle. Moisture evaporated from the timber by a flow of warm air is condensed on the evaporator coils of a refrigeration unit and drained away. The refrigerant is compressed and passed through condenser coils, reheating the air stream.

delamination

the separation of plies or laminations through failure of the bond, visible at an edge.

demos

a term variously used in ancient Greece to describe the citizens, their assemblies, or the lower classes.

density

1. as applied to timber, density is the mass of wood substance and moisture enclosed within a piece expressed in kilograms per cubic meter. As the mass will vary dependant on the amount of moisture in the piece, density is often expressed at a specified moisture content, usually 12%.
2. the mass of substance in a unit volume. When expressed in the metric system, it is numerically equal to the specific gravity of the same substance.

dentil

1. a molding consisting simply of a row of small rectangles resembling teeth (hence, 'dentil'). Normally found in ionic style entablatures under the cornice.
2. square, tooth like molding used frequently in conjunction with a cornice.

dentils

1. are square teeth-like projections that are used to decorate the eaves or roof line of a building.
2. teeth-like ornament used in Classical cornices consisting of a row of evenly spaced, projecting blocks.

depressed arch

a flattened arch, slightly pointed on top. It appears in Late Gothic of the fifteenth and sixteenth centuries. See **arch.** Compare with other types of arches.

depression

the difference between dry and wet bulb temperatures. It is a measure of humidity.

design pressure

specified pressure a product is designed to withstand.

diagonal ribs

the moldings which mark the diagonals in a rib vault. See **rib vault Other types of ribs lierne, ridge, tierceron, transverse.**

diamonding

the change of a square or rectangular section timber to a diamond shape during drying. Diamonding occurs where the growth rings pass through diagonal corners of the section of the piece and is caused by the difference between tangential and radial shrinkage. It is a form of distortion.

diaper

1. a pattern formed by small, repeated geometrical motifs set adjacent to one another, used to decorate stone surfaces in architecture and as a background to illuminations in manuscripts, wall painting or panel painting.
2. a pattern of inscribed squares of diamonds on a wall.

diaper work

decoration of squares or lozenges.

diaphragm

1. wall running up to the roof-ridge.
2. in a beam, an element at right angles to the span with the function of connecting the beams so that they resist load as a unit.
3. a relatively thin, usually rectangular, element of a structure that is capable of withstanding shear in its plane and acts as a bracing elements.

diaphram arch

a transverse, wall-bearing arch that divides a vault or a ceiling into compartments, providing a kind of firebreak.

diazomata

Greek: (diazomata, or katatome) horizontal walkway separating upper and lower sections of cavea seating; corresponds to Roman 'praecinctio'.

diffusion

movement of water through wood from points of high moisture content to points of low moisture content by molecular diffusion.

diffusivity

a measure of the rate of moisture movement through wood by diffusion as a result of differences in moisture content.

dimension

sawn - The nominal dimension of the board plus the over cut to allow for shrinkage.
Nominal - The general intended size of the dry rough sawn board.
Machined - The actual size of a machined or moulded board.

dimension lumber

yard lumber from 2 inches to, but not including, 5 inches thick and 2 or more inches wide. Includes joists, rafters, studs, plank, and small timbers.

dimension stone

historically, the term for large quantities of stone that were cut into large blocks. Dimension stones were used in foundations, piers, and stone-supported walls. It now refers to sized, hewn stone used as exterior facing, or blocks of stone used in windows, arches, chimneys, and other structures. Usually cut into square, rectangular, columnar, tabular, or wedge-shaped blocks.

dimensional change

changes in the size of a piece of dry timber as its moisture content changes to be in equilibrium with the surrounding atmospheric conditions.

dinos

a metal or ceramic container, almost spherical in shape, used by the Greeks for mixing water and wine. The rounded bottom allowed the vessel to sit in a very elaborate, decorated stand, much like a candle sits in a candlestick. An important object in well-furnished Greek homes, a dinos was often illustrated with the favourite mythological stories of its owner.

While many plain, undecorated pots were produced for everyday use, the beautiful, decorated examples were a valuable export item that brought fame to ancient Greece.

■ **dipping**

submerging timber in a dipping vat containing fungicides or other chemicals to prevent stain or decay.

■ **direct nailing**

to nail perpendicular to the initial surface or to the junction of the pieces joined. Also termed face nailing.

■ **discolouration**

change in the colour of wood caused by fungal or chemical stains, weathering, or heat treatment.

■ **displacement**

a change in position. A displacement may be a translation a rotation or a combination of those.

■ **distortion**

1. a drying defect caused by the differential shrinkage along the three axes of a piece of wood. Distortion may take the form of cup, bow, twist, spring or diamonding.
2. alteration of viewed images caused by variations in glass flatness or inhomogeneous portions within the glass. An inherent characteristic of heat-treated glass.

■ **distributed load**

an external force which acts over a region of length, surface, or area essentially any external force which is not a concentrated force.

■ **distyle temple**

having two recessed columns at the front of the temple to form a porch or entrance to the temple.

■ **dog tooth**

an ornamental motif consisting of a square, four-leafed figure, the centre of which projects in a point. It was a very popular in Early English (Early Gothic) architecture. Compare with other repetitive decorative motifs.

■ **dog-legged**

with right-angle bends.

■ **dogtooth**

1. diagonal indented pyramid.
2. characteristic of Early-English period, a decoration consisting of groups of four tooth-like raised pieces set diagonally to each other.

■ **dolly varden siding**

beveled wood siding which is rabbeted on the bottom edge.

■ **domatia**

a room. It refers to small hotels or houses that have inexpensive rooms to rent.

■ **dome**

1. a roof formed by a series of arches, roughly forming a semicircle.
2. a hemispherical vault. See **semi-dome, squinch, pendentive.**
3. rounded, usually hemispherical, vault forming a roof.

■ **domed roof**

a curved roof, frequently used for an atrium or cupola.

■ **domus**

1. the Roman word for house. A single family dwelling like many of those from Pompeii.
2. the ancient Roman word for house. Examples from Pompeii or Ercolano indicate a single story house with a central atrium or courtyard which was

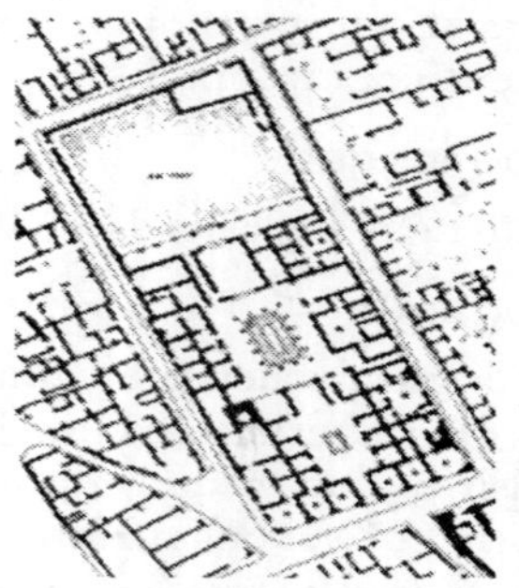

a garden. The larger of these houses may also be referred to as villas. Picture is House of Pansa, Pompeii, Italy.

■ **donjon**

the principal tower of a castle; keep.

■ **donjon or keep**

a freestanding defence tower in a castle complex. Compare with motte-and-bailey.

■ **doorjamb (interior)**

the surrounding case into which and out of which a door closes and opens. It consists of two upright pieces, called side jambs, and a horizontal head jamb.

■ **doric**

1. the most massive and probably the oldest of the orders. The Greek doric had no base, the Romans added one. Shafts are fluted, numbers vary, but there are usually around twenty. The height of the column is between four-and-a-quarter and eight diameters. The entablature is around a quarter of the height of the order. Decoration is copied from timber construction, the cornice projects strongly, the frieze is divided into metopes and triglyphs, the architrave is usually plain.
2. one of three principal styles (or orders) in classical architecture. Doric columns are solid with wide fluting and a plain round capital. They symbolised the male strength.

■ **doric architecture**

the oldest and simplest of the three orders of classical Greek architecture. It is characterised by a column with no base, a Fluted shaft, and a plain Capital.

■ **doric capital**

a simple column top, square in nature. Developed by the Dorian Greeks, however there is a Roman version.

■ **doric column**

is a cylindrical shaft with a square capital or top on the shaft.

■ **doric order**

1. simplest and sturdiest of the three orders; tapering columns rest directly on the stylobate; no base; shallow parallel grooves called

flutes rise from the bottom to the top of the shaft and emphasise its function as a vertical support; sharp ridges divide the flutes; at the top of the shaft a fluted ring called the necking provides a transition to the column's capital; Doric capital consists of a rounded, cushion like element called the echinus, and a horizontal square element called the abacus, which bears the load of the building above.
2. the first and simplest of the three Greek orders and the only one that normally has no base.

■ doric period

the warrior-like Dorians conquered Greece's city-states and created a class of land owning aristocrats from 1100 - 800 BCE. They brought with them iron age technology but also created pottery with geometric designs, thus giving rise to the Geometric Period, also known as the Dark Age, due to the Dorians constant warring and subjugation of the population.

■ dormer

1. a small window projecting vertically from a sloping roof.
2. an opening in a sloping roof, the framing of which projects out to form a vertical wall suitable for windows or other openings.

■ double hung window

a window with two sashes that operate independently of each other and are counterbalanced for opening.

■ double plate

when two layers of 2 x 4's are placed on top of studs in framing a wall.

■ double strength

in float glass, approximately 1/8' (3 mm.) thick.

■ double tree

refers usually to a precast roof deck panel poured with two fins in its underside to impart flexural rigidity.

■ double-glazing

in general, any use of two lights of glass, separated by an air space, within an opening, to improve insulation against heat transfer and/or sound transmission. In insulating glass units the air between the glass sheets is thoroughly dried and the space is sealed, eliminating possible condensation and providing superior insulating properties.

■ double-splayed

embrasure whose smallest aperture is in the middle of the wall.

■ dowel

a cylindrical timber rod or steel bar generally without nut or thread driven into pre-drilled holes to make a joint.

■ dowel joint

a joint where the pieces of timber are joined by dowels running either longitudinally or transversely through the joint.

■ downspout

the metal pipe used to drain water from a roof.

■ **drawbridge**

1. a movable bridge. Early drawbridges were removed horizontally like a gangway.
2. a heavy timber platform built to span a moat between a gatehouse and surrounding land that could be raised when required to block an entrance.

■ **drawing detail**

a top view drawing of a building or roof showing the roof perimeter and indicating the projections and roof mounted equipment, drawn to scale.

■ **drawing outline**

a top view drawing of a building or roof showing only the perimeter drawn to scale.

■ **dressed and matched (tongued & grooved)**

boards or planks machined in such a matter that there is a groove on one edge and a corresponding tongue on the other.

■ **dressed size lumber**

the dimension of lumber after shrinking from green dimension and after machining to size or pattern.

■ **dressed timber**

timber finished to a smooth surface on one or more surfaces.

■ **dressing**

carved stonework around openings.

■ **dressings / accents**

all embracing term, used to describe stones worked to a smooth face and used to form features such as string courses or window margins which contrasts with the surrounding facing material. Dressed stonework is any stone which has been cut to a smooth face. Stone dressings in a brick building are sometimes referred to as 'accents.' Dressing is the cutting, or abrading down of a material to its finished size.

■ **drier paint**

usually oil-soluble soaps of such metals as lead manganese, or cobalt, which, in small proportions, hasten the oxidation and hardening (drying) of the drying oils in paints.

■ **drip**

a member of a cornice or other horizontal exterior finish course that has a projection beyond the other parts for throwing off water. A groove in the under. Side of a sill or drip cap to cause water to drop off on the outer edge instead of drawing back and running down the face of the building.

■ **drip cap**

a moulding placed on the exterior top side of a door or window frame to cause water to drip beyond the outside of the frame.

■ **drip edge**

a device designed to prevent water from running back or under an overhang.

■ **drip mould**

a projection around a window or door with the purpose of channelling water away from the opening.

■ **drippage**

bitumen material that drips through roof deck joints, or over the edge of a roof deck.

■ **drop siding**

1. same as tongue and grove siding. One end of the board has a point (tongue), the other end has a grove. The boards are installed by locking the tongue into the groove.
2. usually ¾ inch thick and 6 and 8 inches wide with tongued-and-grooved or shiplap edges. Often used as siding without sheathing in secondary buildings.

■ **drum**

1. a cylindrical wall which supports a dome.
2. vertical, cylindrical lower part of a dome or cupola.

■ **drum pier**

massive circular support.

■ **drum tower**

1. a large, circular, low, squat tower built into a wall.

■ **dry glazing**

also called compression glazing, a term used to describe various means of sealing monolithic and insulating glass in the supporting framing system with synthetic rubber and other elastomeric gasket materials.

■ **dry rot**

a generic term for the decay of timber by fungi that at an advanced stage leaves the wood light and friable. The term is actually a misnomer as all fungi needs considerable moisture to grow.

■ **dry seal**

accomplishment of weather seal between glass and sash by use of strips or gaskets of Neoprene, EPDM, silicone or other flexible material. A dry seal may not be completely watertight.

■ **dry sheet**

a ply mechanically attached to wood or gypsum decks to prevent asphalt or pitch from penetrating the deck and leaking into the building below.

■ **dryer**

a chamber or apparatus used for drying or conditioning timber or veneer in which the temperature, humidity and velocity of the circulating air are usually controlled.

■ **dry-in**

to make a building waterproof.

■ **drying**

the process of removing moisture from timber to improve its serviceability in use. See **seasoning.**

■ **drying defect**

a feature developing during drying which may decrease the value of a piece of timber.

■ **drying schedule**

a sequence of kiln conditions which result in a gradual decrease in moisture content of the wood.

drystone

unmortared masonry.

drywall

sheetrock (gypsum board) that covers the framing and taping, coating, and finishing to make the interior walls and ceilings of a building. Drywall is also used as a verb to refer to installation process.

dry-wall construction

a type of construction in which the interior wall finish is applied in a dry condition, generally in the form of sheet materials or wood panelling as contrasted to plaster.

drywall hammer

a special hammer used for nailing up gypsum board. It is also known as an axe or hatchet. Edges should be smooth and the corners rounded off. The head has a convex round & checkered head.

drywall nail

nails used for hanging regular drywall that is to be taped and finished later must have adequate holding power and a head design that does not cut the face paper. They must also be of the proper depth to provide exactly 1 inch penetration into the framing member. Nails commonly used are chemically-etched and are designed with a cupped head.

duct

a cylindrical or rectangular 'tube' used to move air either from exhaust or intake, and for distributing warm air from the heating plant to rooms, or air from a conditioning device or as cold air returns. The installation is referred to as 'duct work'.

ductility

ductility generally refers to the amount of inelastic deformation which a material or structure experiences before complete failure. Quantitatively, ductility can be defined as the ratio of the total displacement or strain at failure, divided by the displacement or strain at the elastic limit.

dumbwaiter

an elevator with a maximum footage of not more than 9 sq. ft. floor area; not more than 4' headroom and a maximum capacity of 500 lbs. used for carrying materials only.

dungeon

the jail, usually found in one of the towers.

durability

the natural resistance of timber to biodeterioration due to fungi, insects and mechanical break down caused by weathering, checking and splitting. In building, the efficacy of details in preserving or protecting the fabric of the building from decay or deterioration.

durability class

durability is expressed as one of four classes. The value for each species is based on trials of the resistance to both decay and termites of untreated heartwood in the ground. The classes are: Class 1- Timber of the highest natural durability, expected to have a life of at least 25 years and up to 50 years in the ground. Class 2 - Timber of high natural durability, expected to have a life of about 15 to 25 years in the ground. Class 3 - Timber of moderate natural durability, expected to have a life of about 8 to 15 years in the ground. Class 4 - Timber of low durability, expected to have a life of 1 to 8 years in the ground. The sapwood of all species is regarded to be Class 4.

■ **durometer**

the measurement of hardness of a material. A gauge to measure the hardness of an elastomeric material.

■ **Dutch colonial revival**

19th and 20th century architecture based on earlier colonial examples from the 17th and 18th century. The style typically features a gambrel roof, often with flared eaves, a Dutch door, double hung windows and decorative shutters. With barns, the form is much simpler with the dominant feature the gambrel roof.

■ **Dutch door**

a door that is divided in two with the ability to open the top and bottom parts separately.

■ **dynamic equilibrium**

equilibrium which includes inertial forces.

■ **early English**

earliest phase of Gothic building, around 1175-1265, typified by plain, clean designs and lancet windows. Salisbury is a good example.

■ **early English style**

the beginnings of Gothic in England span from the final years of the twelfth century through the first half of the thirteenth. Cathedrals primarily constructed within this period are Canterbury, Wells, Lincoln and Salisbury. Within each of these, excepting perhaps Salisbury, it is plain to recognise preceding Romanesque forms and elements. Image at right: Salisbury cathedral, England.

■ **earlywood**

the less dense, larger celled, first formed part of a growth ring. Also called 'springwood'.

■ **east end**

refers to the end of the church where the main altar is placed and where the main part of the service takes place. Generally, medieval churches were oriented toward the east. However, topography of the land or other factors may have prevented an absolute east- west orientation for a church. The term east end, is generally used to describe the area where the main altar is placed in a medieval church, even in those cases where the church is not oriented exactly toward the east. Contrast with west end

■ **eave**

the part of a roof which projects out from the side wall, or the lower edge of the part of a roof that overhangs a wall.

■ **eaves**

1. the under part of a sloping roof that hangs over a wall.

2. the point where the roof projects from the wall of a building.

eccentric load

loads that are applied off the central axis of a structural member.

ecclesia

personification of Church. Often appears with Synagoga (Personification of Judaism) Personifications of the Church (Ecclesia) and Judism (Synagoga). Both appear as female figures- Ecclesia was crowned and holding a chalice and Synagoga was blindfolded and held the Tablets of the Law (the Ten Commandments given to Moses).

echinus

a convex moulding forming part of the capital in doric and ionic orders, below the abacus.

eclectic

composed of many architectural styles.

eco labelling

eco labelling is a form of third party certification of a product that confirms that the product meets particular environmental criteria. Eco labels are designed to help consumers choose products that do less damage to the environment. Criteria for a product group are generally developed by the application of a life cycle assessment approach.

ecological consequences

ecology is defined as the study of the interrelations between living organisms and their environment, including both physical and biotic factors. Therefore ecological consequences refers to the changes the environmental effect may have on the relationships between living organisms and their environment.

ecologically sustainable forest management

integrating commercial and non-commercial values of forests so that the welfare of society (both material and non-material) is improved, whilst ensuring that the values of forests, both as a resource for commercial use and for conservation are not lost or degraded for current and future generations.

ecosystem

a natural system that functions as unit. It is assemblage of living organisms together with their non-living environment in a particular area. Healthy ecosystems are necessary for maintaining and regulating: atmospheric quality, climate, fresh water, marine productivity, soil formation, cycling of nutrients and waste disposal.

edge bedding

occurs where the layers of the stone are vertical and run at 90 degrees to the plane of the wall. Projections such as cornices and pediments should be edge bedded. Increasingly, the French term *en delit* is used to describe this technique, which neatly avoids the confusion which can arise when the natural layers of the stone are described as beds, and the stones themselves are usually laid in the horizontal mortar joints, universally referred to as beds.

■ **edge clearance**

nominal spacing between the edge of the glass product and the bottom of the glazing pocket (channel.)

■ **edge grain (vertical)**

edge-grain lumber has been sawed parallel to the pith of the log and approximately at right angles to the growth rings; i.e., the rings form an angle of 45° or more with the surface of the piece.

■ **edge metal**

a term relating to brake or extruded metal around the perimeter of a roof.

■ **EER**

Energy Efficiency Ratio; is figured by dividing BTU hours by watts.

■ **efflorescence**

the process by which water leeches soluble salts out of concrete or mortar and deposits them on the surface. Also used as the name for these deposits.

■ **egg and dart**

1. a repetitive decorative motif often used in classical antiquity and copied in the Middle Ages. It consisted of oval (egg-shaped) motifs alternating with dart-like motifs.
2. a moulding consisting of an arrow-like element alternating with an egg-shaped element.

■ **egg and tongue**

a moulding consisting of a egg-shaped element alternating with a downward pointing tongue. Easily confused with egg and dart.

■ **EIFS**

Exterior Insulating and Finish System; exterior wall cladding system consisting primarily of polystyrene foam board with a textured acrylic finish that resembles plaster or stucco.

■ **elastic**

a material or structure is said to behave elastically if it returns to its original geometry upon unloading.

■ **elastic limit**

the point beyond which the deformations of a structure or material are no longer purely elastic.

■ **elastomer**

an elastic rubber-like substance, such as natural or synthetic rubber.

■ **elastomeric**

of or pertaining to any of the numerous flexible membranes that contain rubber or plastic.

■ **electrodes**

pins or blades on electric moisture meters, usually made of steel, used to penetrate and contact the wood. Insulated - Electrodes that are coated with an insulating material to limit or control the point of contact between the electrode and the wood.

■ **electrolytic coupling**

a fitting required to join copper to galvanised pipe and gasketed to prevent galvanic action. Connecting pipes of different materials may result in electrolysis.

■ **elevation**

1. a side of a building. The front elevation is the facade (face) of a building. Elevations are usually associated with a compass direction for clarity (such as 'northeast elevation'.)
2. a drawing of the walls of one side of a building, either interior or exterior, with all lines drawn to a scale to show true vertical and horizontal dimension; also used in reference to the vertical plane of a building, as in the 'west elevation'.

■ **embattled**

battlemented; crenelated.

■ **emblem**

the Athens 2004 Olympic Games' emblem is an olive wreath - the 'kotinos' with which the Olympic winner was crowned in classical times. It is a symbol linked with the Olympic ideals, peace and the city of Athens, whose sacred tree was the olive tree. Its circular shape projects universal meanings of the unity of the world, the circle of life and the link between time past and present.

■ **embodied energy**

all of the energy invested in bringing a material to its final product, including transportation.

■ **embodied energy**

the amount of non-renewable energy used to extract and process raw materials into finished building components. The embodied energy of a material is usually expressed in the units MJ/kg and that of a sheet building component or element MJ/m2.

■ **embrasure**

1. the low segment of the altering high and low segments of a battlement.
2. a splayed opening in a wall that enframes a doorway or a window.

■ **emissivity**

the measure of a surface's ability to emit long-wave infrared radiation.

■ **e-modulus**

see **modulus of elasticity.**

■ **EMT (Electrical Metallic Tubing)**

this electrical pipe, also called thinwall conduit, may be used for both concealed and exposed areas. It is the most common type of raceway used in single family and low rise residential and commercial buildings.

■ **emulsion**

in roofing, a coating consisting of asphalt and fillers suspended in water.

■ **enceinte**

the enclosure or fortified area of a castle.

■ **end coating**

a coating of moisture-resistant material applied to the end grain of green logs or sawn boards to slow end drying.

end dams

internal flashing (dam) that prevents water from moving laterally within a curtain wall or window wall system.

end grain

the grain shown on a cross cut surface.

end lap

the amount or location of overlap at the end of a roll of roofing felts in the application.

energy

a property of a body related to its ability to move a force through a distance opposite the force's direction; energy is the product of the magnitude of the force times the distance. Energy may take several forms. See **kinetic energy, potential energy, and elastic energy.**

engaged shaft

a shaft set into a wall or larger shaft.

engineered lumber

recycled or reconstituted wood materials, which employ laminated wood chips or strands and finger-jointing (gluing large pieces together.)

English / Norman cottage

generally a small house of masonry or frame construction with simple floor plans. Considered picturesque because of their setting in the surrounding environment.

engraving

print made from an engraved plate.

entablature

1. architectural element consisting of three parts: an architrave (plain horizontal beam resting on columns), a frieze (decorative panel or relief), which corresponded to the beams supporting the ceiling, and a cornice (a set of decorative moldings that overhangs the parts below).
2. the upper horizontal part of an order, between a capital and the roof; it consists of the architrave, frieze, and cornice.
3. in classical architecture, the beam-like division above the columns, comprising architrave, frieze and cornice.
4. the part of a classical temple above the columns between a Capital and the roof. It consists of the Architrave, Frieze and Cornice.
5. an elaborate molding band found in Neoclassical/Classical Revival, supported by columns. The molding includes a cornice, a frieze (often dentil molding) and an architrave (generally un ornamented). Columns support the entablature.
6. a thing of significance about which information needs to be known or held.

environmental audits

environmental audits are a useful management tool that may form part of an overall environmental management system. This process entails a systematic and objective evaluation of how the organisation is performing in relation to its policies, regulatory requirements, environmental management systems and practices.

■ **environmental impact assessments**

environmental impact assessments predict environmental impacts of a new development at the design stage.

■ **environmental impacts**

the environment is defined as the physical and chemical surroundings of an object, the cultural, aesthetic and other factors which contribute to quality of life. Therefore environmental impacts refers to the effects on the surroundings, primarily physical things.

■ **environmental management systems**

environmental management systems are systems that ensure the organisation is working within the framework of ecologically sustainable development.

■ **EPDM**

Ethylene Propylene Diene Monomer. A single ply membrane consisting of synthetic rubber; usually 45 or 60 mils. Application can be ballasted, fully adhered or mechanically attached.

■ **episkenion**

the facade of the second story of the Greek skene; pierced by one or more doors (thyromata), the episkenion served as a background for performances with the roof of the proskenion serving as a stage.

■ **epoxy dowel joint**

a joint in which the parts are joined by dowels that have been set in oversized holes with epoxy resin.

■ **epoxy resin joint**

a joint in which the parts are bonded using an epoxy resin adhesive.

■ **equalisation**

in kiln drying, a high humidity treatment in the final stages of drying intended to reduce the moisture content range between pieces of timber and the moisture gradient within pieces of timber. Also known as equalising.

■ **equilibrium moisture content**

the moisture content at which timber neither gains nor loses moisture from the surrounding atmosphere.

■ **estiatorio**

literally a restaurant. They are usually more formal and more expensive than a Taverna but offer a more formal standard of eating.

■ **evangelist symbols**

symbols for the authors of the four New Testament books which are narratives of the life of Christ. These symbols were very common in manuscripts, sculpture and wall paintings, especially form the Early Medieval through the Romanesque periods.

■ **evzones**

named for the small village of Evzoni in northern Greece, these guards stand watch over the Tomb of the unknown solider in front of the parliament building in downtown Athens.

■ **excavate**

dig the basement and or all areas that will need footings/foundations below ground.

■ **excavation**

the process of methodically unearthing buried objects from a piece of land to learn about the past.

■ **exedra**

1. a semicircular niche or hemicycle.
2. an often semicircular Portico with seats that was used in ancient Greece and Rome as a place for discussions.

■ **expansion coefficient**

the amount that a specific material will vary in any one dimension with a change of temperature.

■ **expansion joint**

a device used to permit a structure to expand or contract without breakage. In residential construction, a bituminous fibre strip used to separate blocks or units of concrete to prevent cracking due to expansion as a result of temperature changes. Also used on concrete slabs.

■ **exterior glazed**

glazing infills set from the exterior of the building.

■ **exterior plywood**

plywood of naturally durable or treated veneers bonded with waterproof adhesive and capable of withstanding prolonged exposure to severe exterior conditions without failure of the glue-lines.

■ **exterior stop**

the molding or bead that holds the light or panel in place when it is on the exterior side of the lite or panel.

■ **external force**

a surface force or body force acting on an object. External forces are sometimes called applied forces.

■ **extractives**

1. substances such as tannin in wood that are not an integral part of the cellular structure and can be removed in solution by solvents, such hot or cold water, that do not react chemically with wood substances.
2. small amount of substances additional to the major components of wood which give timbers their own colour and odour. Resin is the best known.

■ **extrados**

outer curve of the voussoirs.

■ **extrusion**

an item formed by forcing a base metal (frequently aluminium) or plastic, at a malleable temperature, through a die to achieve a desired shape.

■ **eyebrow**

1. a dormer whose roof line is an arch curve that flattens out to the horizontal plane of the roof; shaped like an eyebrow.

2. a flat, normally concrete, projection which protrudes horizontally from a building wall; Eyebrows are generally located above windows.

facade

1. any important face of a building, usually the principal front with the main entrance.
2. the main face or elevation of a building. From the French word meaning 'front' or 'face.'
3. the front of a building. Frequently, in architectural terms an artificial or decorative effort.
4. usually, the front of a building; also the other sides when they are emphasised architecturally.

face bedding

occurs where the layers of the stone are vertical and parallel to the plane of the wall. Usually leads to extensive powdering and scaling of the stone.

face brick

brick made especially for exterior use with special consideration of colour, texture and size, and used as a facing on a building.

face glazing

a system having a triangular bead of compound applied with a putty knife, after bedding, setting, and clipping the glazing infill in place on a rabetted sash.

face nailing

nailing at right angles to the surface.

facing

a covering applied to the outer surface of a building. Facing is usually both functional and decorative. Stone facing or modern siding provides extra warmth, but also looks pretty.

false front

the extension vertically of the facade of a building above the roofline to give the illusion that the building is taller than it actually is.

fan light

a circular window over a door, often with a patter that suggests a fan.

fan vault

1. a vault which consists of fan-shaped half cones which usually meet at the centre of a vault. other types of vaults net vault, barrel, groin, quadripartite, sexpartite.
2. a Perpendicular vault, typified by large carved fan-shaped details. Found at Gloucester (Choir and Cloister) and Peterborough (retrochoir.)

fan vault is

a development of lierne vaulting characteristic of English Perpendicular Gothic, in which radiating ribs form a fan-like pattern.

fascia

1. a vertical board nailed to the lower ends of rafters.
2. a moulding simply of a thin, blank band.
3. a plain horizontal band in an architrave.
4. in residential construction, a flat board, band, or face, used sometimes by itself but usually in combination with mouldings, often located at the outer face of the cornice. Any cover board or framed metal assembly at the edge or eaves of a flat, sloping, or overhanging roof, which is placed in a vertical position to protect the edge of the roof assembly.

fascine

huge bundle of brushwood for revetting ramparts or filling in ditches.

fasteners

a general term covering a wide variety of screws and nails, which may be used for mechanically securing various components of a building.

fauces

a small entry room of a Roman house, just as one enters the front door. Leads to atrium.

feature

any irregularity or imperfection in a tree, log, board, or other wood product. Feature may result from knots and other growth conditions and abnormalities, insect or fungus attack, or during timber processing.

felt

a very general term used to describe composition of roofing ply sheets, consisting of a mat of organic or inorganic fibres unsaturated, impregnated with asphalt or coal tar pitch, or impregnated and coated with asphalt.

fenestration

1. the arrangement of the windows of a building.
2. the arrangement of windows and openings in a building.
3. any glass panel, window, door, curtain wall or skylight unit on the exterior of a building.
4. the general term used to denote the pattern or arrangement of openings, i.e. windows and doors, etc, in a facade.

feng shui

translates literally to 'wind-water'. Feng Shui is the ancient Chinese art of placement. The goal of Feng Shui is to achieve harmony, comfort, and balance, first in ones environment and then in one's life.

ferrous

refers to objects made of or partially made of iron, such as ferrous pipe.

■ **fibre**

small diameter, thick walled cells in hardwoods. Fibres dominate the structural behaviour of hardwoods.

■ **fibre saturation point**

the point in the seasoning or wetting of timber at which the cell cavities are free from water but cell walls are still saturated with bound water. It is taken as approximately 25-30% moisture content.

■ **fibreboard**

a generic term including sheet materials of widely varying densities manufactured from refined or partially refined wood or vegetable fibres. Bonding agents and other materials may be added to increase strength or to improve other properties.

■ **fiddleback**

figure in timber or veneer produced by small, regular undulations in the grain.

■ **fieldstone**

stone found in nearby fields or rock formations that are large enough for construction use. The stones usually have an irregular shape.

■ **figure**

the pattern produced on the cut surface of wood by annual growth rings, rays, knots, deviations from regular grain such as interlocked and wavy grain, and irregular coloration.

■ **figured or historiated capital**

a capital which is decorated with figures of animals, birds, or humans, used either alone or combined with foliage. The figures need not have any meaning, although they may be symbolic or part of a narrative sequence. Historiated capitals were most commonly used in the Romanesque from the late eleventh to mid-twelfth centuries. See **capital, figured or historiated initial, other types of capital figured or historiated initial an illuminated initial containing a figure, a group of figures, or a narrative scene, illuminated initial, figured or historiated capital**

■ **fillet**

narrow flat band.

■ **fillet bead**

caulking or sealant placed in such a manner that it forms an angle between the materials being caulked.

■ **finger joint**

an end joint in which wedge shaped projections in one piece of timber fit matching recesses on the other piece and are bonded together by an adhesive.

■ **finial**

1. a slender piece of stone used to decorate the tops of the merlons, spire, tower, balustrade, etc.

2. an ornament at the tip of a pinnacle, spire or other tapering vertical architectural element. See **also spire, pinnacle. fleur-de-lis stylised lily which served as symbol for the French monarchy. Compare with Tudor Rose.**
3. a decorative ornament that tops off the crest of a gable, tower, or other architectural element.
4. Fish scale shingles that are rounded on one end and then installed overlapping to give a fish scale appearance.

finish

in hardware, metal fastenings on cabinets which are usually exposed such as hinges and locks.

finish carpentry

the hanging of all interior doors, installation of door molding, base molding, chair rail, built in shelves, etc.

finish coat

the last coat applied in plastering intended as a base for further decorating or as a final decorative surface. Finish coat usually consists of calcified gypsum, lime and sometimes an aggregate. Some may require the addition of lime or sand on the job. The three basic methods of applying it are (1) trowel (2) flat and (3) spray.

finish grade

any surface which has been cut to or built to the elevation indicated for that point. Surface elevation of lawn, driveway or other improved surfaces after completion of grading operations.

fire rated

descriptive of materials that has been tested for use in fire walls.

fire retardant chemical

a chemical or preparation of chemicals used to reduce flammability or to retard spread of flame.

fire stop

a solid, tight closure of a concealed space, placed to prevent the spread of fire and smoke through such a space. In a frame wall, this will usually consist of 2 by 4 cross blocking between studs.

fire wall

any wall built for the purpose of restricting or preventing the spread of fire in a building. Such walls of solid masonry or concrete generally sub-divide a building from the foundations to two or more feet above the plane of the roof.

fire-resistive

in the absence of a specific ruling by the authority having jurisdiction, applies to materials for construction not combustible in the temperatures of ordinary fires and that will withstand such fires without serious impairment of their usefulness for at least 1 hour.

fish tape (fish wire)

material used to advance wire through a conduit.

fishplate

a wood or plywood piece used to fasten the ends of two members together at a butt joint with nails or bolts. Sometimes used at the junction of opposite rafters near the ridge line.

■ fixed connection

in two dimensions, a fixed connection between two members restrains all three degrees of freedom of the connected member with respect to one another. A fixed connection is sometimes called a rigid connection or moment-resisting connection.

■ fixed support

in two dimensions, a fixed support restrains three degrees of freedom two translations and one rotation.

■ flagstone (flagging or flags)

flat stones, from 1 to 4 inches thick, used for rustic walks, steps, floors, and the like.

■ flake

a scale-like particle. To lose bond from a surface in small thin pieces. Sometimes a paint film 'flakes'.

■ flamboyant style

the closing period of French Gothic during the late fourteenth and early fifteenth centuries. A style characterised by tracery designs which resemble upward spiralling flames, dominant in the north of France. A classic example of this work is the north spire of Chartres which stands in evident contrast to the remainder of the cathedral, completed two centuries before.

■ flange

in beams, the longitudinal ribs of a built up member primarily intended to resist flexure. The flanges are joined by a web.

■ flash point

the critical temperature at which a material will ignite.

■ flashing

1. a strip of impervious material fitted to provide a barrier to moisture movement into the interior of a building.
2. weatherproof material installed between roof sheathing (or wall sheathing) and the finish materials to help keep moisture away from the sheathing. Typically, sheet metal or a similar material is used in roof and wall construction to protect a building from water seepage.

■ flat glass

a general term that describes float glass, sheet, glass, plate glass, and rolled glass.

■ flat grain

flat-grain lumber has been sawed parallel to the pith of the log and approximately tangent to the growth rings, i.e., the rings form an angle of less than 45° with the surface of the piece.

flat paint
an interior paint that contains a high proportion of pigment and dries to a flat or lustreless finish.

flat seam
a seam at the junction of sheet metal roof components that has been bent at the plane of the roof.

flattened hipped roof
a hipped (pyramidal) roof that is flat at the top instead of pointed.

fleche
slender wooden spire rising from a roof. The word is French for 'arrow'.

fleet averaging
by using a point system, builders can show compliance with energy building requirements by using average figures for all air conditioning units in the same sub division.

flexibility
flexibility is the inverse of stiffness. When a force is applied to a structure, there is a displacement in the direction of the force; flexibility is the ratio of the displacement divided by the force. High flexibility means that a small load produces a large displacement.

flexible metal conduit
conduit similar to armoured cable in appearance but does not have the pre-inserted conductors.

flexural strength
the resistance at failure of a beam subjected to bending.

flexure
bending deformation, i.e., deformation by increasing curvature.

flitch
a large piece of log, sawn on at least two surfaces, intended for further cutting.

float glass
glass formed on a bath of molten tin. The surface in contact with the tin is known as the tin surface or tin side. The top surface is known as the atmosphere surface or air side.

floor board
boards dressed to standard thickness and generally finished with a tongue and groove, fixed to floor joists or a substrate to provide a floor.

floor plan
the basic layout of building or addition, which includes placement of walls, windows and doors as well as dimensions.

floor plan or ground plan
horizontal cross-section of a building as the building would look at ground level. A ground plan shows the basic outlined shape of a building and, usually, the outlines of other interior and exterior features. Compare with cross section.

floor plate
see **floor plan.**

flooring
the covering of internal floors in a building. Timber flooring includes tongue and groove strip

flooring, parquetry, panel flooring, particleboard and plywood.

■ **flue**

the space or passage in a chimney through which smoke, gas, or fumes ascend. Each passage is called a flue, which together with any others and the surrounding masonry make up the chimney.

■ **flue lining**

fire clay or terra-cotta pipe, round or square, usually made in all ordinary flue sizes and in 2-foot lengths, used for the inner lining of chimneys with the brick or masonry work around the outside. Flue lining in chimneys runs from about a foot below the flue connection to the top of the chimney.

■ **flush glazing**

(pocket glazing) The setting of a light of glass or panel into a four-sided sash or frame opening containing a recessed 'U' shaped channel without removable stops on three sides of the sash or frame and one channel with a removable stop along the fourth side.

■ **flute (or fluting)**

vertical channelling, roughly semicircular in cross section and used principally on columns and pilasters.

■ **fluted**

a style of architecture where a column has vertical indentations.

■ **fluting**

1. concave mouldings in parallel.
2. shallow, concave grooves running vertically on a column, pilaster, or other surface. See **also column, shaft, pier, pilaster**

■ **fly ash**

a product of coal burning that makes concrete stronger.

■ **fly rafters**

end rafters of the gable overhang supported by roof sheathing and lookouts.

■ **flying buttress**

1. a supporting structure composed of a pillar with an arch stretching to a wall that the buttress provides support for. Popular in the Gothic period.
2. a free-standing buttress attached to the main vessel (nave, choir, or transept wall) by an arch or half-arch which transmits the thrust of the vault to the buttress attached to the outer wall of the aisle.
3. arch conveying the thrust of a vault towards an isolated buttress.
4. typically consists of an inclined member carried on an arch or a series of arches and a solid buttress to which it transmits lateral thrust.

■ **folded plate**

the configuration of flat sheets, such as plywood, into a folded form to produce a beam of considerably higher strength and stiffness than is possible with the flat sheet alone.

■ **folded seam**

in sheet metal work, a joint between sheets of metal wherein the edges of the sheets are crimped together and folded flat.

■ **foliate capital**

a capital decorated with foliage elements. See **column, pier, capital.**

■ **foliate initial**

an illuminated initial filled with decoration in leaf scroll. See **illuminated initial, foliate capital Other types of illuminated initial historiated, inhabited, pen flourished.**

■ **foliated**

carved with leaves.

■ **folly**

purely decorative building, without function, such as the Gothic ruins built to romanticise parks and gardens in 18th century England.

■ **font**

a receptacle for water, used for baptism. See **baptistery.**

■ **foot print**

see **floor plan.**

■ **footings**

1. bottom part of wall.
2. wide pours of cement reinforced with re-bar (reinforcing bar) that support foundation walls, pillars, or posts. Footings are part of the foundation and are often poured before the foundation walls.

■ **force**

a directed interaction between two objects that tends to change the momentum of both. Since a force has both direction and magnitude, it can be expressed as a vector.

■ **force system**

see **system of forces.**

■ **forebuilding**

an extension to the keep, guarding it's entrance.

■ **forest**

an area incorporating all living and non-living components that is dominated by trees usually with a single stem and a mature or potentially mature stand height exceeding five metres. The existing or projected foliage cover of over storey strata should be equal to or greater than 30 percent.

■ **forest estate**

all forests growing on public or private lands

■ **forest practices**

forest practices means the processes involved in establishing forests, or growing or harvesting timber, and includes the construction of roads; and the development and operation of quarries; and other works connected with establishing forests, or growing or harvesting timber

■ **forgery**

a false imitation of something.

■ **form**

the shape or structure of a city, a building, or a part of a building. Two examples of easily recognisable building forms are the courtyard or skyscraper.

■ **formal**

the qualities in architecture related to form and usually following convention or rules.

■ **fornix**

older Roman term for an arch. Used also as a description of an arch which is flanked by engaged columns which in turn support an entablature above the arch.

■ **fortress church**

a church built so that it might be used for defensive purposes.

■ **forum**

1. main square or marketplace of a Roman town. In Roman towns in Greek lands, the Greek term agora is often used instead. The forum was often surrounded by the most important governmental institutions such as a curia building, temple to Jupiter Capitolium, basilica or other such structures.
2. the open air urban space(s) in ancient Roman cities, generally rectangular in shape, defined by the porticoes and civic buildings at its perimeter, and used for marketplace and public interaction, particularly 'civic discussion'. The temple stood prominently at one end of the forum. above picture is Plan of the Forum, Pompeii.

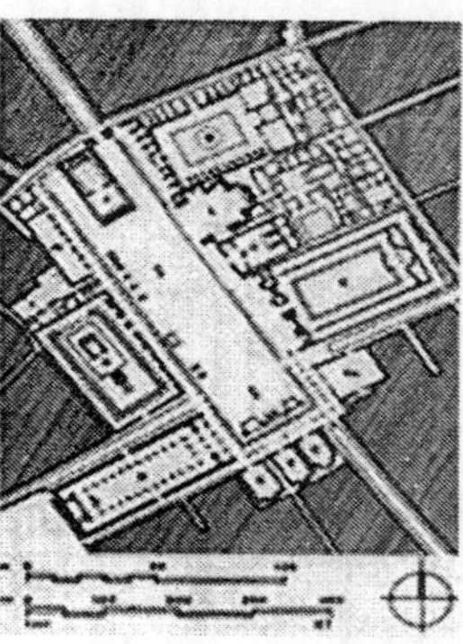

■ **fosse**

ditch.

■ **foundation**

1. the soil, subsoil or rock upon which a structure is supported.
2. the supporting portion of a structure below the first floor construction, or below grade, including the footings.

■ **frame**

the main timbers of a structure fitted and joined together. A three dimensional self contained structural system of interconnecting members which functions with or without the aid of horizontal diaphragms or floor bracing systems.

■ **frame structure**

a structure built from wood studs that form a framework that carries the load of a building to the ground. Frame buildings have an exterior sheathing of wood, masonry, tin or other materials.

■ **framing timber**

timber used to form the basic structure of a building, such as studs and joists.

■ **frappe**

considered by some as the national drink of modern Greece, most Greeks drink at least one a day. It is a cold, frothy mixture of instant coffee, water, and optionally, milk and sugar.

■ **free moisture**

moisture which is present in the cell cavities of wood.

■ free stuff

timber with no knots or other imperfections.

text

natural language prose, often unstructured. In an automated system, free-text fields are for qualification and display of the contents of separate fields designated as access points. See **descriptive category.**

■ freestone

high-quality sandstone or limestone.

■ fresco

1. painting on wet plaster wall.
2. wall painting applied to plaster when it is wet. Frescoes were popular in may warm countries until the Middle Ages.

■ frieze

1. the middle part of an entablature, often decorated with spiral scrolls (volutes).
2. decorated central division of an entablature, between the architrave and the cornice.
3. the section of an entablature between the cornice and the architrave. It can be decorated with continuous reliefs (as in Ionic), divided into metopes and triglyphs (as in Doric), or left plain or filled with an inscription (as in the Corinthian favorued by the Romans.)
4. a deep band of decorative sculpture running along the upper part of a wall.
5. a horizontal sculptured part of an Entablature that is above the Architrave and below the Cornice.
6. the middle division of the Classical entablature found below the cornice and above the architrave. Also a band below a cornice, which may or may not be decorated.
7. in house construction a horizontal member connecting the top of the siding with the soffit of the cornice.

■ frigidarium

the cooling off pool in a Roman Bath complex (do not confuse with natatio.)

■ FRL

Fire Resistance Level - grading periods in minutes of the fire resistance of building elements for structural adequacy/integrity/and insulation.

■ frostline

the depth of frost penetration in soil. This depth varies in different parts of the country. Footings should be placed below this depth to prevent movement.

■ fully tempered glass

flat or bent glass that has been heat-treated to a high surface and/or edge compression. Fully tempered glass, if broken, will fracture into many small pieces (dice) which are more or less cubical. Fully tempered glass is approximately four times stronger than annealed glass of the same thickness when exposed to uniform static pressure loads.

■ fully-adhered

a completely attached (adhered) roof membrane.

■ **function**

the particular use or purpose for which the structure was built, and can be either pragmatic, symbolic, or both.

■ **funerary**

of or for a funeral.

■ **fungi (wood)**

microscopic plants that live in damp wood and cause mold, stain, and decay.

■ **fungicide**

a chemical that is poisonous to fungi.

■ **fungus (fungi)**

a plant that feeds on wood fibre. Fungi primarily consist of microscopic threads (hyphae) that traverse wood in all directions, dissolving materials out of the cell walls.

■ **funicular**

a funicular shape is one similar to that taken by a suspended chain or string subjected to a particular loading.

■ **furnace**

a heating system that uses the principle of thermal convection. When air is heated, it rises and as the air cools it settles. Ducts are installed to carry the hot air from the top of the furnace to the rooms. Other ducts, called cold air returns, return the cooler air back to the furnace.

■ **furring**

strips of wood or metal applied to a wall or other surface to even it and normaliy to serve as a fastening base for finish material.

■ **gable**

1. wall covering end of roof ridge. 2. the end of a building as distinguished from the front or rear side. The triangular end of an exterior wall from the level of the eaves to the ridge of a double-sloped roof. In house construction, the portion of the roof above the eave line of a double-sloped roof.

■ **gable end**

an end wall having a gable.

■ **gable(d)**

the exterior, usually triangular, wall segment under a ridged roof.

■ **gabled roof**

a roof that slopes on two sides of a central ridge.

■ **galilee**

a structure at the West end of the church, adjoining the West Front, either a porch (as at Ely) or a chapel (as at Durham.)

■ **gallery**

long passage or room.

■ **gallery or tribune**

an upper story over the aisle which opens onto the nave or choir. It corresponds in length and width to the dimensions of the aisle below it. Contrast with triforium. See **aisle, clerestory.**

■ **galley**

a long passage or room.

■ **galvanise**

to coat a metal with zinc by dipping it in molten zinc after cleaning.

■ **gambrel roof**

1. a roof which has two pitches on each side.
2. a type of roof which has its slope broken by an obtuse angle, so that the lower slope is steeper than the upper slope.

■ **garderobe**

a small latrine or toilet either built into the thickness of the wall or projected out from it, projects from the wall as a small, rectangular bartizan.

■ **gargoyle**

a spout placed on the roof gutter of a Gothic building to carry away rainwater, commonly carved fancifully as in the shapes of animal heads.

■ **garth**

the area bounded by the Cloister.

■ **gaskets**

pre-formed shapes, such as strips, grommets, etc., of rubber or rubber-like composition, used to fill and seal a joint or opening either alone or in conjunction with a supplemental application of a sealant.

■ **gate house**

the complex of towers, bridges, and barriers built to protect each entrance through a castle or town wall.

■ **gauge**

the thickness of sheet metal and wire, etc.

■ **gauge board**

(spot board) Board used to carry grout needed to patch small jobs.

■ **general contractor**

(prime contractor) A contractor responsible for all facets of construction of a building or renovation.

■ **genuine**

authentic.

■ **geodesic**

the shortest line between two points on a surface, such that a geodesic dome is segmented into a series of straight elements.

■ **geometric period**

the period from 1200 - 800 BCE. is also called the Dark Age. The period is named for pottery decorated with geometric designs that was made by the ruling and warring Doric civilisation.

■ **georgian**

the prevailing style of English architecture during the reigns of George I, II, and III (1714- 1820), based on the principles of the Italian Renaissance architect Andrea Palladio. The style was transported to England by Inigo Jones and Sir Christopher Wren. It became the prototype for the colonial style in America.

■ **georgian revival**

also referred to as Colonial Revival, a style that was popular from 1870s until the turn of the century. Georgian revival is based on British architecture popular during the reign of King George IV (1714-1830). The style is symmetrical, with some of the features being a pedimented front gable, hipped roof clad in slate, Palladian windows, pediments over the main doorway and decorative pilasters.

■ **GFRC**

Glass Fibre Reinforced Concrete; Material used in wall systems that resembles but generally does not perform as well as concrete. Usually a thin cementations material laminated to plywood or other lightweight backing.

■ **gibbs surround**

the framing of a door or window by a head composed of a (usually triple) keystone and by jambs that are bordered by protruding rectangular blocs of stone.

■ **gingerbread**

1. carved and pierced wooden ornament often found on Victorian houses. So named because of the resemblance to sugar-frosted decoration on gingerbread cookie houses.

■ **girder**

a main beam upon which floor joists rest used to support concentrated loads at isolated points along its length, usually made of steel or wood.

■ **glacis**

a bank sloping down from a castle which acts as a defence against invaders; broad, sloping naked rock or earth on which the attackers are completely exposed.

■ **glass**

a hard, brittle substance, usually transparent, made by fusing silicates under high temperatures with soda, lime, etc.

■ **glaze coat**

in roofing, a light, uniform mopping of bitumen on exposed felts to protect them from the weather, pending completion of the job.

■ **glazing**

a generic term used to describe an infill material such as glass, panels, etc. The process of installing an infill material into a prepared opening in windows, door panels, partitions, etc.

■ **glazing bead**

in glazing, a strip surrounding the edge of the glass in a window or door which holds the glass in place.

■ **glazing channel**

in glazing, a three-sided, U-shaped sash detail into which a glass product is installed and retained.

■ **gloss (paint or enamel)**

a paint or enamel that contains a relatively low proportion of pigment and dries to a sheen or lustre.

■ **gloss enamel**

a finishing material made of varnish and sufficient pigments to provide opacity and colour, but little or no pigment of low opacity. Such an enamel forms a hard coating with maximum smoothness of surface and a high degree of gloss.

glue

an animal, mineral or vegetable adhesive.

glue laminated timber

laminated timber where the laminations are joined with adhesive.

gothic

1. a style employed in Europe during the thirteenth, fourteenth, and fifteenth centuries; also called pointed. It is characterised by the use of pointed arches and ribbed vaults, piers, and buttresses in the support of its stone construction. The style is best exemplified by the Notre Dame in Paris and the cathedrals of Amiens and Bourges.
2. period of building from 1200-1550, typified by pointed-topped arches. Three main periods can be identified: early english, decorated and perpendicular.

gothic art

seldom separated from the building craft of the Cathedrals, the term is used loosely to refer to religious European art forms of the 12th through 16th centuries. Other mediums utilised extensively during this period, and within similar manner, were Painting, Tapestry, Metalwork, Glasswork and Manuscript Illumination.

gothic revival

architectural style based of the original Gothic period in the European Middle Ages. The revival style features pointed arches in window and door openings, tracery in windows, battlements, vaults, cross gables and ornate decoration. Gothic Revival was particularly popular with churches and university buildings (Collegiate Gothic) and homes (Carpenter Gothic.)

grade

the designation of the quality of a piece of timber or other manufactured wood products in accordance with standard rules.

grade MW

Moderate Weather grade of brick for moderate resistance to freezing used, for example, in planters.

grade NW

no Weather brick intended for use as a back-up or interior masonry.

grade SW

severe Weather grade of brick intended for use where high resistance to freezing is desired.

gradus

Latin: step or position Roman cavea seats; according to Vitruvius the gradus, 'are not to be less than twenty inches in height, nor more than twenty-two. Their width must not be more than two feet and a half, nor less than two feet.'

grain

the general direction of the fibres or wood elements relative to the main axis of the piece. The direction, size, arrangement, appearance, or quality of the fibres in wood or timber Across the Grain - The direction parallel with the length of the fibres and other longitudinal elements of the wood. Along the Grain - the direction at right angles to the length of the fibres and other longitudinal elements of the wood. Coarse - timber with wide conspicuous growth rings in which there is considerable difference between earlywood and latewood. The term is sometimes used to designate wood with large vessels, but in this sense the term 'coarse textured' is more often used closed - timber with narrow, inconspicuous growth rings. The term is sometimes used to designate wood having small and closely spaced vessels, but in this sense the term 'fine textured' is more often used. Cross - timber in which the fibres deviate from a line parallel to the sides of the piece. Cross grain may be either diagonal or spiral grain or a combination of the two. Diagonal - timber in which the annual rings are at an angle with the axis of a piece as a result of sawing at an angle with the bark of the log. A form of cross grain. End - the grain of the ends of logs or timber on a cross cut surface. Interlocked - timber in which fibres are inclined in one direction in a number of rings of annual or seasonal growth, then reverse and are inclined in an opposite direction in succeeding growth rings. Irregular - grain where the fibres contort and twist around knots, butts, curls and so on. Also called wild grain. Open - common classification for woods with large vessels in the grain. Also known as coarse textured or coarse grained. Raised - roughened surface of timber and other wood products, particularly softwood, after planning, caused by the projection of earlywood or latewood above the surface. Slope of - in timber and other wood products, the ratio of deviation of the grain from the long axis of a piece to the distance along the edge that this deviation occurs. Spiral - a form of cross grain in timber in which the fibres take a spiral course about the trunk of a tree instead of the normal vertical course. The spiral may extend in a right handed or left-handed direction around the tree trunk. Straight - timber in which the fibres and other longitudinal elements run parallel to the axis of a piece.

■ granules

the mineral particles of a graded size which are embedded in the asphalt coating of shingles and roofing.

■ gravel

loose fragments of rock used for surfacing built-up roofs, in sizes varying from 1/8' to 1 3/4'.

■ gravity

an attractive force between two objects; each object accelerates at a rate equal to the attractive force divided by the object's mass. Objects near the surface of the earth tend to accelerate toward the earth's centre.

■ grey water

wastewater produced from baths and showers, clothes washers, and lavatories sometimes used for irrigation.

■ great chamber

lord's solar, or bed-sitting room.

■ great hall

the building in the inner ward that housed the main meeting and dining area for the castle's residence; throne room.

■ Greek cross

1. a cross with four arms of equal length. Compare with Latin cross. 2. A floor plan with four equal wings surrounding a square centre. The building looks like a plus sign from above.

■ Greek key or meander

an ornamental motif consisting of continuous bands arranged in rectilinear forms. See **other repetitive decorative motifs**

■ green building

this is a loosely defined collection of land-use, building design, and construction strategies that reduces undesirable environmental impacts. Benefits of building green include reduced energy consumption, protection of ecosystems, and occupant health.

■ green timber

unseasoned timber, with free moisture present in the cell cavities.

■ griffin

mythical animals with the body of a lion and the head of an eagle. They were mainly known in Anatolia from where they passed into the Minoan, and from there to ancient Greek mythology and art.

■ grillage

a system of orthogonal elements, usually beams or trusses, acting together to resist a common load.

■ grisaille

greyish glass, ornamented with monochrome enamel.

■ groin vault

a vault produced by the intersection at right angles of two barrel (tunnel) vaults. Sometimes the arches of groin vaults may be pointed instead of round. See **barrel vault.**

■ groin vault types of barrel vault

longitudinal,

■ groined

roof with sharp edges at intersection of cross-vaults.

■ groined vault

1. a vault comprising the intersection of two tunnel vaults, no ribs. 2. a rib-less vault formed by the meeting of a pair of equal barrel vaults at right angle to each other.

■ grotesque

a marginal figure or animal, or hybrid combination of human and animal or plant, frequent especially in Gothic manuscript illumination and especially in marginal illumination

■ ground plan or floor plan

horizontal cross-section of a building as the building would look at ground level. A ground plan shows the basic outlined shape of a building and, usually, the outlines of other interior and exterior features.

■ ground system

the connection of current-carrying neutral wire to the grounding terminal in the main switch which in turn is connected to a water pipe. The neutral wire is called the ground wire.

■ grounding rod

rod used to ground an electrical panel.

■ grounds

1. guides used around openings and at the floor line to strike off plaster. They can consist of narrow strips of wood or of wide subjambs at interior doorways. They provide a level plaster line for installation of casing and other trim. 2. an aggregate of items that share a common history. Groups are defined by repositories, and they often have several subgroups established according to archival principles of provenance. A catalogue record will correspond to one level of a group, be it the top or whole group or one of the parts, such as a series.

■ grout or grouting

a cement mortar mixture made of such consistency (by adding water) that it will just flow into joints and cavities of masonry work to fill them solid.

■ growth rings

rings of earlywood and latewood on the transverse section of a trunk or branch marking cycles of growth.

■ guilloche

a decorative molding, usually used circled around the top of a column base, of plaited or braided elements.

■ gum

a natural exudation, also called kino, produced in trees as a result of fire or mechanical damage.

■ gum vein

a ribbon of gum between growth rings, which may be bridged radially by wood tissue at intervals. Also known as kino.

■ gun consistency

sealant formulated in a degree of viscosity suitable for application through the nozzle of a caulking gun.

■ gunite

a construction material composed of cement, sand or crushed slag and water mixed together and forced through a cement gun by pneumatic pressure, used in the construction of swimming pools.

■ gusset

a flat wood, plywood, or similar type member used to provide a connection at intersection of wood members. Most commonly used at joints of wood trusses. They are fastened by nails, screws, bolts, or adhesives.

■ gusset plate

plates, often steel or plywood, fixed by nails, bolts or other means to connect timber members in a truss or other frame structure. Gusset plates may be applied to one or both sides of a joint.

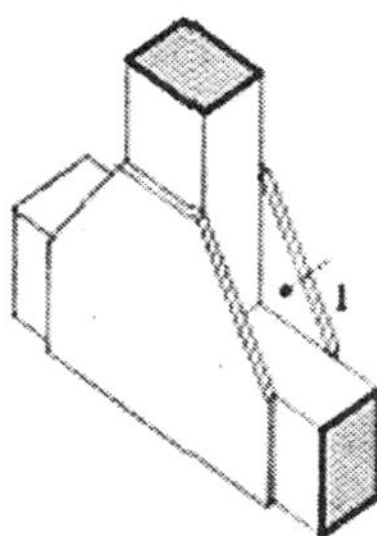

■ **guttae**

1. small projections under the triglyphs in a doric frieze. Said to represent pegs used in the original timber construction.

■ **gutter**

metal or wood trough at the eaves of a roof to carry rain water from the roof to the downspout.

■ **gutter strap**

metal bands used to support the gutter.

■ **guy wire**

a strong steel wire or cable strung from an anchor on the roof to any tall slender projection for the purpose of support.

■ **gymnasium**

a derivative of the word gymnos - nude. It was a place comprising sports grounds and buildings (including baths) where athletes exercised naked.

■ **gypsum board**

see **drywall.**

■ **gypsum keene cement**

material used to obtain a smooth finish coat of plaster, for use over gypsum plastic base coats only and in areas not subject to moisture. It is the hardest plaster.

■ **gypsum plaster**

gypsum formulated to be used with the addition of sand and water for base-coat plaster.

■ **half-shaft**

roll-moulding on either side of opening.

■ **half-timber**

the common form of medieval construction in which walls were made of a wood frame structure filled with wattle and daub.

■ **hall**

1. the principal room in the complex used for receiving guests and for a major entertainments.

■ **hall curch (or hallenkirch)**

popular in Germany, a church with aisles the same height as the nave, and no clerestory. (Bristol is one.)

■ **hammer**

a tool consisting of a metal head set perpendicular on a handle, used for driving nails.

■ **hammer beams**

right angled support beams projecting from wall tops to brace wooden roofs.

■ **hardboard**

a pressed homogenous fibreboard having a mean density of not less than 800 kg/sq m.

■ **hardness**

a property of wood that enables it to resist indentation. It is measure in kN and is often determined by the Janka hardness test.

■ hardware

metal accessories such as door knobs, towel bars, toilet paper holders, etc.

■ hardwood

a general term for timber of broad leafed trees classified botanically as Angiosperm. The term has no reference to the relative hardness of the wood.

■ harvested rainwater

rainwater captured and used for indoor needs, irrigation, or both.

■ hatch

an opening in a deck; floor or roof. The usual purpose is to provide access from inside the building.

■ haunch

1. the part of an arch at which the lateral thrust is strongest.
2. the lower section of the arch, below the crown, where outward thrust is most pronounced.

■ hawk

a flat wood or metal tool 10 inches to 14 inches square with a handle used by plasterers to carry plaster mortar or mud.

■ hazard insurance

insurance for a building while it is under construction.

■ HCFC

Hydro Chloro Fluoro Carbon, a chemical compound used in aerosol cans.

■ header

framing members over windows, doors, or other openings. A beam placed perpendicular to joists and to which joists are nailed in framing for chimney, stairway, or other opening. A wood lintel.

■ hearth

the inner or outer floor of a fireplace, usually made of brick, tile, or stone.

■ heartwood

the wood making up the centre part of the tree, beneath the sapwood. Cells of heartwood no longer participate in the life processes of the tree. Heartwood may contain phenolic compounds, gums, resins, and other materials that usually make it darker and more decay resistant than sapwood.

■ heat strengthened glass

flat or bent glass that has been heat-treated to a specific surface and/or edge compression range. Heat-strengthened glass is approximately two times as strong as annealed glass of the same thickness when exposed to uniform static pressure loads. Heat-strengthened glass is not considered safety glass and will not completely dice as will fully tempered glass.

■ heel bead

sealant applied at the base of a channel, after setting the light or panel and before the removable stop is installed, one of its purposes being to prevent leakage past the stop.

heliocaminus

room in a Roman bath complex with large, thermal windows used to gather heat from the sun.

Hellenistic period

from 338 - 146 BC. Greece expanded its influence over a large area. Phillip II of Macedonia began by taking over Greece and the city-states that were rundown from the many wars during the Classical Period. After his assassination, his son Alexander the Great conquered Syria, Palestine, Egypt (where he founded Alexandria), Persia, northern Afghanistan, and northern India thus spreading 'Hellenism' throughout a great area. After Alexander's death his conquered territories were divided and weakened, thus ushering in the period of Roman control.

hermetic seal

vacuum seal (between panes of a double-paned window i.e. insulated glass unit or IGU.) Failure of a hermetic seal causes permanent fogging between the panels of the IGU.

heroon

a temple or funerary monument dedicated to a hero, the offspring of a god and a human.

herringbone

brick or stone laid in alternate diagonal courses.

hewn timber

timber with or without wane, finished to size with hand tools such as an axe or adze.

hexastyle temple

having a portico of six columns at either end.

high altar

a large church may have several altars. The term high altar refers to the main altar in the chancel. Other altars may be located on the sides of the nave or in separate chapels in the same building.

high-early cement

a portland cement sold as type III sets up to its full strength faster than other types.

hillfort

bronze or iron age earthwork defences of concentric ditches and banks.

himation

outer cloak worn by ancient Greeks. This garment was traditionally pulled under the right arm and draped over the left shoulder.

hip roof

a roof that rises by inclined planes from all four sides of a building.

hip

the external angle formed by the meeting of two sloping sides of a roof.

hip rafter

a rafter that forms the intersection of an external roof angle.

hipped roof

1. a roof with sloped instead of vertical ends.

2. a roof with a pyramid shape. The roof meets all four walls of a building.

■ hippodamian system

a form of ancient city building with a grid of parallel streets and residential blocks of the same size, called insulate.

■ historic floor plan

as viewed by a worshiper seated among the congregation, there are two speaker's stands on either side of the front of the church. The one on the left is called the pulpit, and clergy to read the gospel lesson and to preach the sermon uses it. Accordingly, the left side of the church is called the gospel side. The on the right is called the lectern. It generally holds a large Bible and is used by lay readers for the Old Testament and epistle lessons. Accordingly, the right side of the church is called the epistle side. The communion table stands centred behind the lecterns and is surrounded by a kneeling rail. If there is enough room, the communion table is placed away from the wall so that the celebrant may face the congregation during communion. To receive communion, the congregation comes up and kneels at the rail. The choir may be located behind the congregation, to one or both sides of the sanctuary, or even on the opposite side of the communion table from the congregation. The choir is most often not in direct sight of the congregation. The wall that the congregation faces during worship is called the 'east wall' regardless of the actual compass direction, because of the ancient practice, inherited from Judaism, of facing Jerusalem during prayers. Orthodox churches follow this plan, with some elaboration. Many Roman Catholic churches use a variation of the historic plan, in which the nave is semi-circular or circular, surrounding the chancel.

■ hit and miss

areas on dressed or moulded boards that that are not fully machined. It results form unacceptable unevenness in the thickness or width of the boards. It is also called skip.

■ hoarding

upper wooden stories on a stone castle wall; the living area; sometimes, a temporary wooden balcony suspended from the tops of walls from which missiles could be dropped.

■ hobnail

a pattern of pin-holes left by insect attack.

■ hoistway

a shaft way for the travel of one or more elevators.

■ hollow-cast

made through a process that leaves something empty on the inside.

■ honeycomb

areas in a foundation wall where the aggregate (gravel) is visible. Honeycombs can be usually be remedied by applying a thin layer of grout or other cement product over the affected area. Method by which concrete is poured and not puddled or vibrated, allowing the edges to have voids or holes after the forms are removed.

■ honeycombing

a drying defect which occurs when tensile stresses in the core (usually a result of collapse) result in the formation of internal cavities.

■ hood

1. arched covering; when used as umbrella, called hood-mould.
2. an arched covering; when used to throw off rainwater, called hood-mould.

■ hora

the generic name for the main town on a Greek island, regardless of the town's actual name. Therefore, nearly every island in Greece has a town called Hora.

■ horizontally laminated timber

laminated timber designed to resist bending loads applied perpendicular to the wide face of the laminations. For vertical loads, this means that the wide face runs horizontally.

■ hornwork

freestanding quadrilateral fortification in front of the main wall.

■ horrea

Roman warehouse.

■ housed joint

a joint where one piece is notched or grooved to receive the other piece.

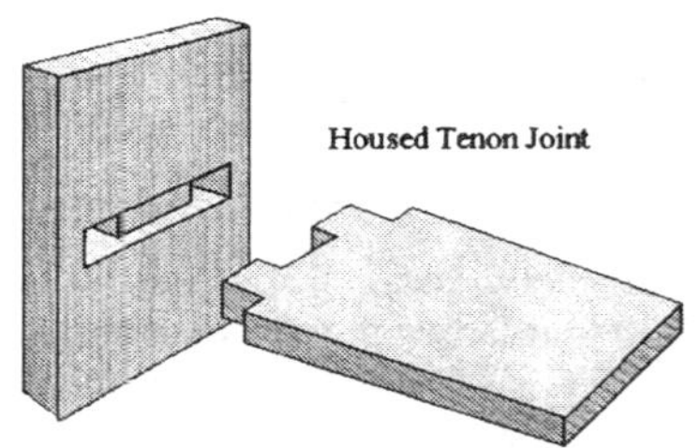

■ hub

in plumbing, the enlarged end of a pipe which is made to provide a connection into which the end of the joining pipe will fit.

■ humidifier

a device designed to increase the humidity within a room or a house by means of the discharge of water vapour. They may consist of individual room size units or larger units attached to the heating plant to condition the entire house.

■ humidistat

a device for automatically regulating the relative humidity of air.

■ humidity

a general term for the presence of water vapour in air. There is a known limit to the amount of water vapour that air can hold at any particular temperature. Absolute - the amount of moisture in air. It is usually expressed as the weight of water vapour in a unit weight of dry air relative at a given temperature, this is the amount of moisture in air as a percentage of the maximum moisture carrying capacity of the air.

■ **HVAC**

Heating Ventilation and Air Conditioning.

■ **hydroelectric elevator**

an elevator where liquid is pumped under pressure directly into the cylinder by a pump driven by an electric motor without an accumulator between the pump and cylinder.

■ **hydronic heating**

in-floor hot water heating system where hot water is pumped through a thermal mass floor which absorbs the heat and evenly radiates the over an extended period of time.

■ **hydropower**

hydropower is the production of electricity by harnessing the power of flowing water, usually through the use of a waterwheel.

■ **hygrometer**

an instrument for measuring the humidity of air.

■ **hygroscopic**

changes its moisture content to be in equilibrium with the atmosphere.

■ **hygrostat**

a device for automatically regulating the equilibrium moisture content of the air. See **humidistat.**

■ **hyperbolic paraboloid shell**

a complex curved surface which has one line which is always straight.

■ **hyperoon**

the area above the side Nave of a temple. In the Hellenistic basilica the Hyperoon was above the side Nave and the Narthex, from where the women watched the service, giving this area the name gynaikonite or women's nave.

■ **hypocausts**

small column-like elements used to support a floor in the caldarium of a Roman bath complex. Hot air from a furnace is pumped into the spaces around the hypocausts and under the floor, thus heating the floor and/or the water above.

■ **hyposkenion**

see **proskenion.**

■ **hysteresis**

as applied to timber's moisture content, the tendency of dried wood to reach equilibrium with any specified temperature and relative humidity at a lower moisture content when absorbing moisture from a drier state than when losing moisture from a wetter state.

■ **I-Beam**

a steel beam with a cross section resembling the letter I. It is used for long spans as basement beams or over wide wall openings, such as a double garage door, when wall and roof loads are imposed on the opening.

■ **icon**

a religious picture painted in oil on a small wooden panel. They are venerated in the Greek Orthodox religion.

■ iconostasis

an altar screen or partition embellished with icons running across an entire end of a church. At first, an iconostasis was just a small wall that served as a symbolic marker of the division between the Sanctuary and the Nave, or between the heaven and the earth. Icons were placed on the small wall and eventually several rows were permanently installed, thus creating the wall seen today.

■ illuminated initial

in manuscript illumination, a highly ornamented letter, usually the first letter of a word. Types of illuminated initial foliate, historiated, inhabited, pen flourished impost block or abacus The slab at the top of a capital between the capital and the architectural member above. See **column, pier, other parts of a column or pier capital, shaft, column base infilling or webbing.** The vault surface between the ribs of a rib vault. Compare with rib

■ ima cavea

Latin: deepest or bottommost theatre seating, lowest tier of cavea seating - most desirable seating, reserved for the more distinguished.

■ impluvium

in the atrium of a Roman house, the depression in the floor below the compluvium or opening in the roof which lets rainwater in. The water collects in the impluvium.

■ impost

1. a wall bracket to support an arch.
2. projection marking the point from which the arch springs from its support.

■ incompatibility

descriptive of two or more materials which are not suitable to be used together.

■ inelastic

not surprisingly, the opposite of elastic. A deformation of a structure or material under load is described as inelastic when the deformation remains after the load is removed. The term plastic is often used with the same meaning.

■ infection

the invasion of timber by fungi or other microorganisms.

■ infestation

the establishment of insects or other animals in timber.

■ infiltration

the process by which air leaks into a building. In either case, heat loss results.

■ inhabited initial

an illuminated initial containing animals or human figures such as naked fighters. See **illuminated initial other types of illuminated initial foliate, historiated, pen flourished**

■ inlay

a material, such as glass or stone, that is set into the surface of another material.

inner curtain

the high wall the surrounds the inner ward.

inner ward

the open area in the centre of a castle.

INR

Impact Noise Rating. A single figure rating which provides an estimate of the impact sound insulating performance of a floor-ceiling assembly.

inside drain

in roofing, a drain positioned on a roof at some location other than the perimeter. It drains surface water inside the building through closed pipes to a drainage system.

insula

1. the building type from the ancient Roman society made up of a block with shops and light industry at the ground level and apartments above. These structures ranged in height from four to seven stories.
2. an apartment style building with many domestic units. Sometimes term is also used by archaeologists to refer simply to a room designated by ruined walls.

insulating glass unit

two or more lights of glass spaced apart and hermetically sealed to form a single-glazed unit with an air space between each light. (Commonly called IG units.)

insulation

generally, any material which slows down or retards the flow or transfer of heat. Building insulation types are classified according to form as loose fill, flexible, rigid, reflective, and foamed-in-place. All types are rated according to their ability to resist heat flow (R-Value.)

insulation board

a rigid structural building board made of coarse wood or cane fibre in ½ and 25/32-inch thickness It can be obtained in various size sheets, in various densities, and with several treatments.

insulation fasteners

any of several specialised mechanical fasteners designed to hold insulation down to a steel or a nailable deck.

interior finish

material used to cover the interior framed areas, or materials of walls and ceilings.

interior glazed

glazing infills set from the interior of the building.

interlace

a decorative motif consisting of threads passing aver and under each other like threads in lace.

interlayer

in glazing, any material used to bond two lights of glass and/or plastic together to form a laminate.

interlocked grain

grain where the angle of the fibres periodically changes or reverses in successive layers.

internal force

forces which hold an object together when external forces or other loads are applied. Internal forces are sometimes called resisting forces since they resist the effects of external forces.

internal hinge

see **pin connection.**

interply

between two layers of roofing felts that have been laminated together.

intersecting arches

arches which cross over each other in an arcade See **arcade, blind arcade.**

intrados

inner face of voussoirs.

ionic

1. later than the doric, the ionic order has a distinctive capital, with two volutes, and an echinus based on a water lily shape. The Greek capital was straight sided, the volutes on the Roman capital angled outwards. The columns, on attic bases, usually have about twenty four flutes, and are between eight and nine diameters in height. The entablature is usually about one-fifth of the whole. The cornice projects and often has dentil ornamentation, the frieze can be decorated, the architrave is usually divided into three fascias.

2. one of three principal styles (or orders) in classical architecture. Ionic columns are slender with narrow fluting and a scrolled capital. They symbolise the female shape, as opposed the Doric which symbolises the male shape.

ionic architecture

one of the three orders of classical Greek architecture that was neither simple nor ornate.

ionic capital

a capital used originally by the Greeks in a system of supports called the Ionic order. In the medieval period, the capital was often used without a strict adherence to the rest of the system. An Ionic capital has a volute, or a spiral scroll-like carving, on each side as its major decoration. Ionic capitals are relatively rare in medieval buildings.

ionic column

1. is a cylindrical shaft with a scroll shaped top on the shaft.
2. a column, frequently fluted (grooved), with a capital in a scroll shape.

ionic order

distinguished from the doric primarily by its column and frieze; Ionic column rests on an elaborate curving base rather than directly on the stalemate; column shaft usually has deeper flutes and is more slender than the doric; height-to-base ratio of early Ionic columns was 8 to 1, compared with a ratio between 4 to 1 and 6 to 1 for doric columns; typical Ionic capital has two spiral volutes, elements that resemble partly unrolled scrolls; Ionic capital looks different from the sides than from the front or back causing problems in columns that stood at the corners, where volutes had to slant at a 45-degree angle so that their spiral pattern would look the same from the front of the temple as from the sides.

IRMA

Insulated (or inverted) Roof Mem Brane Assembly. In this system the roof membrane is laid directly on the roof deck, covered with extruded foam insulation and ballasted with stone, minimum of 1000 lbs. per square.

irregular courses

when stone or brick are laid in a seemingly random fashion.

irregular grain

grain where the fibres contort and twist around knots, butts, curls and so on. Also called wild grain.

iso 14000 - environmental management standards

ISO 14000 is a series of international, voluntary environmental management standards developed by the International Organisation for standardisation to provide organisations with a common framework for managing environmental issues.

isotropic

exhibiting the same properties in all directions.

Italian renaissance revival

1. architectural style found in the 1800s through the 1930s, and popular with Beaux-Arts school architects. Features include smooth stone used on the first floor, windows and doors with voussoirs, corner quoins, a different fenestration for each floor, false balconies with balustrades, massive elaborate cornice and decorative detailing.
2. any physically integral item, such as a drawing, volume, document, sheet, or sketchbook.

itinera versurarum

outer two door openings of the five doors in a Roman scaenae frons: doors in the Roman versurae (section of the scaenae that flanks the stage.)

jack rafter

a rafter that spans the distance from the wall plate to a hip, or from a valley to a ridge. A rafter that spans the distance from the wall plate to a hip, or from a valley to a ridge.

jamb

1. side posts of arch, door, or window.
2. a vertical element of a doorway or window frame. See **trumeau, jamb figures.**
3. the vertical side masonry of a door, window or portal entranceway, often a place for the setting of statuary. Image at right: Jamb Statuary within the west portal at Rheims in France.

jamb figures

statues carved on the jambs of a doorway or window. Jamb statues were often human figures- either religious figures or secular or ecclesiastical leaders.

jig

a device used to set a dimension, angle or shape for fabrication.

joggled

keyed together by overlapping joints.

joinery

finished timber fixtures of buildings such as doors, windows, panelling, cupboards, etc.

joint

1. a prepared connection for joining pieces of wood or veneer.
2. the space between the adjacent surfaces of two members or components joined and held together by nails, glue, cement, mortar, or other means.

joint cement

a powder that is usually mixed with water and used for joint treatment in gypsum-wallboard finish. Often called 'spackle.'

joint group

species of timber are classified into joint groups according to their mechanical properties. There are six joint groups for unseasoned timber (J1, the strongest to J6, the weakest) and six joint groups for seasoned timber (JD1 to JD6.)

joist

1. wall-to-wall timber beams to support floor boards.
2. one of a series of timber beams used to support the floor boards or ceiling of a building.
3. one of a series of parallel beams, usually 2 inches in thickness, used to support floor and ceiling loads, and supported in turn by larger beams, girders, or bearing walls.

kafeneio

a smoky, dimly lit, male-only coffee house where men spend the day playing cards, backgammon, smoking, and drinking coffee.

kafeteria

today the best translation would be cafe or coffee shop. Rarely do they serve food, but Greeks manage to spend several hours at them drinking coffee, chatting with friends, and people watching.

■ kastro

a castle or walled-in town.

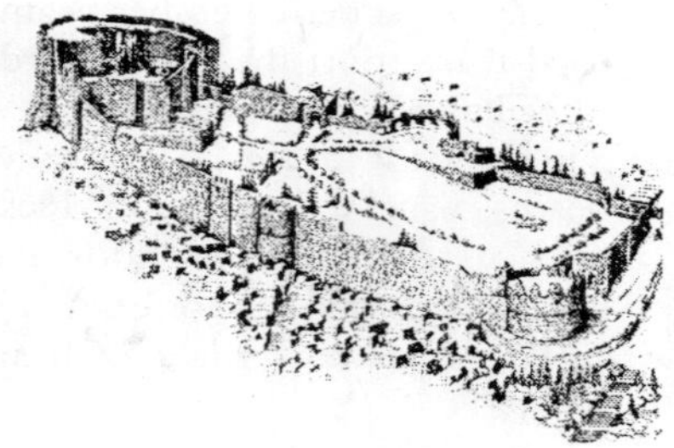

■ katholikon

the main church of a monastery.

■ keene's cement

a white finish plaster that produces an extremely durable wall. Because of its density, it excels for use in bathrooms and kitchens and is also used extensively for the finish coat in auditoriums, public buildings, and other places where walls may be subjected to unusually hard wear or abuse.

■ keep

the strongest tower of a castle. Usually where the lord lived.

■ keep or donjon

a freestanding defence tower in a castle complex. Compare with motte-and-bailey

■ kekrides

Greek name for wedge shaped seating section in cavea; (also: kerkis); corresponds to Roman 'cunei'.

■ kerf

the cut made by a saw blade.

■ kerfing

making a series of parallel saw cuts part way through the thickness of a piece of timber so that the piece can be curved towards the kerfed side.

■ kerkis

Greek name for wedge shaped seating section in cavea; (also: kekrides); corresponds to Roman 'cunei'

■ keystone

1. central wedge in top of arch.
2. the voussoir at the top of an arch; in vaulting it occurs at the intersection of the ribs of a rib vault. It is important structurally since it marks the apex of the vault.
3. central, wedge-shaped stone of an arch, so called because the arch cannot stand up until it is in position.
4. the central, uppermost part of an arch.
5. a wedge shaped masonry element typically found over the centre of a window or door. In an arch, keystones help support the weight of the structure above.

■ kick hole

a defect frequently found in perimeter flashings arising from being stepped on or kicked. A small fracture of the base flashing in the area of the cant.

■ kick plate

a protective element added to doors and the areas below windows, primarily in commercial buildings, to avoid marring the surface underneath.

■ **kiln**

a chamber used for seasoning timber in which the temperature and humidity of the circulating air can be controlled.

■ **kiln dried lumber**

lumber that has been kiln dried often to a moisture content of 6 to 12 percent. Common varieties of softwood lumber, such as framing lumber are dried to a somewhat higher moisture content.

■ **kiln-dried**

dried artificially in a kiln.

■ **klimakes**

Greek stairway in caveat.

■ **knee brace**

a diagonal corner brace fastened between a column and a beam or truss to provide lateral restraint.

■ **kneeler**

in churches where it is customary to kneel for prayer, there is often a long, narrow padded bar at the base of pew in front of you, which can be tilted down for kneeling and tilted up to make it easier to get in and out of the pew. Most often the kneelers are the length of the pew and are used by several people. If you are visiting a church that has kneelers, and you are not accustomed to using them, keep the kneeler in the down position during the service except while someone is passing through. Otherwise someone might attempt to kneel when the kneeler isn't in place. See also **prayer desk.**

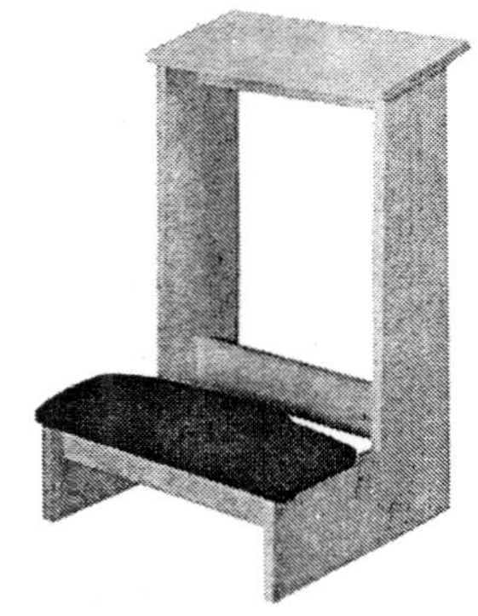

■ **knife consistency**

compound formulated in a degree of firmness suitable for application with a putty knife such as used for face glazing and other sealant applications.

■ **knot**

1. that portion of a branch or limb that has been surrounded by subsequent growth of the stem. The shape of the knot as it appears on a cut surface depends on the angle of the cut relative to the long axis of the knot.
2. a knot is formed when a branch becomes embedded in the trunk. While they can increase the resistance of timber to splitting, they can seriously effect the bending strength of joists, floorboards etc.
3. In lumber, the portion of a branch or limb of a tree that appears on the edge or face of the piece.

■ **kore**

female statues of the Archaic period, the male versions were called Kouros.

■ **kore**

an ancient Greek statue of a young woman. Pl. Korai.

■ **kouros**

statues of the archaic period that were symmetrical stiff standing males, the female representations were called Kore.

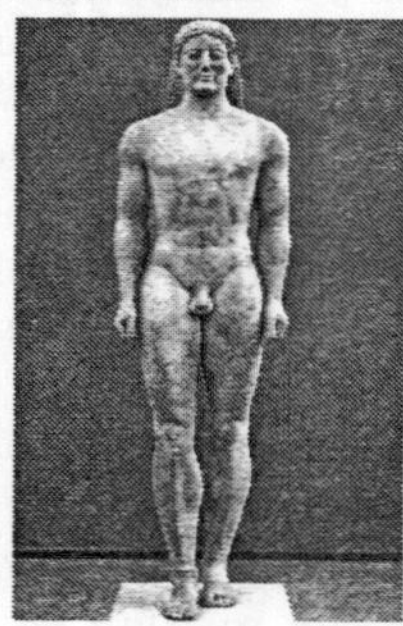

■ **kouros**

an ancient Greek statue of a young man. Plu. Kouroi

■ **kraft**

a heavy, water resistant paper.

■ **kynar coating**

architectural coating that is UV stable and suitable for exterior use on aluminium and other metal surfaces.

■ **labelling**

labelling is a term used to describe the use of a label or certification mark that indicates that the timber product has been produced from a certified forest and the chain of custody verified. Labelling in this way relates only to the how the timber has been grown and manufactured, not the quality of the product or its fitness for purpose.

■ **laconicum**

hot, dry room of a roman bath complex.

■ **ladder, fixed**

a ladder which is permanently attached to a building.

■ **lady chapel**

a chapel dedicated to the Virgin Mary. May be situated at the rear of the church, east of the retro choir (Wells) or elsewhere (Ely.)

■ **laminated glass**

two or more lights of glass permanently bonded together with one or more inter-layers.

■ **laminated timber**

a built up product made of layers or laminations of wood, all with the grain laid parallel and glued or otherwise fastened together. Laminating timber allows large and structurally reliable sections to be built up from small, high quality pieces

Laminated Veneer Lumber (LVL)

a structural lumber manufactured from veneers laminated into a panel with the grain of all the veneers running parallel to each other.

lancet

1. a tall narrow, pointed window.
2. long, narrow window with pointed head.
3. a slender, pointed window. See **mullion**

lancet window

window with a single, sharply pointed arch. The style is associated with the early english

period of Gothic architecture, around the 13th century.

land use change and forestry

land use change and forestry is an overarching title used internationally for sources (emissions) and sinks (removals) associated with the following activities: Forestry - commercial harvesting, fuel wood consumption, & incremental growth of managed forests and plantations; & land use change - loss of above ground biomass, onsite and off-site burning of above ground biomass, decay of above ground biomass, soil disturbance, and sequestration in post burning re-growth.

landing

a platform between flights of stairs or at the termination of a flight of stairs.

lantern

1. small structure with open or windowed sides on top of a roof or dome to let light or air into the enclosed space below.
2. a small circular or polygonal structure, with windows all around the base, which opens above a larger tower or dome. Latin cross :A cross with three short arms and one long arm. Compare with Greek cross

lantern tower

a tower with a lantern on top, so that light may enter the church via the tower windows.

lap

to extend one material partially over another; the distance so extended.

lap joint

a joint made by placing one member partly over another and bonding the overlapped portions.

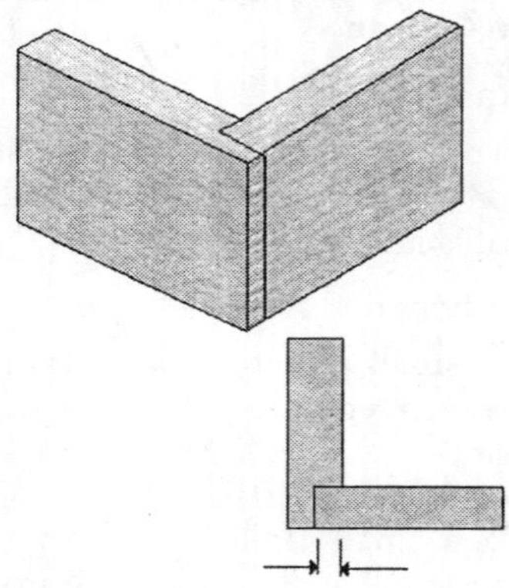

lap siding

same as clapboard siding, used to clad a structure by overlapping boards.

lararium

the shrine area in a roman house, usually at the back, where household gods are worshipped and their images housed.

lateral force

a force applied horizontally to a structure in any direction, such as a force caused by wind or earthquake action.

lateral movement

movement in a structure that is perpendicular to the major axis of loading, i.e. usually horizontal movement.

lateres

roman bricks. These could be fired clay (*coctus*) or simply dried mud like adobe (*crudus*).

latewood

the denser wood formed during the later stages of growth of each annual ring. Also called 'summerwood'.

lath

a building material of wood, metal, gypsum, or insulating board that is fastened to the frame of a building to act as a plaster base.

lattice

laths or lines crossing to form a network.

lattice window (clathri window)

windows that have wood or

metal strips that divide glass in a diagonal pattern to create an ornamental effect.

layout

within an air-drying yard, layout refers to the arrangement of timber stacks in the yard.

lead

a malleable metal once extensively used for flashings.

■ leader

see **downspout.**

■ lean-to roof

the sloping roof of a building addition having its rafters or supports pitched against and supported by the adjoining wall of a building.

■ lectern

in churches with a historic floor plan, there are two speaker's stands in the front of the church. The one on the right (as viewed by the congregation) is called the lectern. The word lectern comes from the Latin word meaning 'to read,' because the lectern primarily functions as a reading stand. It is used by lay people to read the scripture lessons, except for the gospel lesson, to lead the congregation in prayer, and to make announcements. Because the epistle lesson is usually read from the lectern, the lectern side of the church is called the epistle side. See **ambo and pulpit.** In some churches, the positions of the pulpit and the lectern are reversed (that is, pulpit is on the right and the lectern is on the left) for architectural or aesthetic reasons.

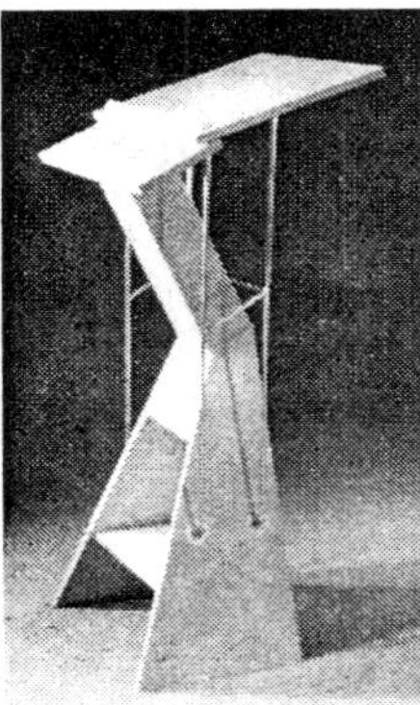

■ lecture-hall floor plan

as viewed by a worshiper in the congregation, there is one speaker's stand, cantered in the front of the church. It is technically an ambo, but is often incorrectly called the pulpit. It is used by all individuals who are involved in the conduct of the worship service. The choir is seated behind the pulpit, facing the congregation and in full view. There is usually a long kneeling rail between the congregation and the pulpit. If there is a communion table, it is located between the kneeling rail and the pulpit. To receive communion, the congregation comes up and kneels at the rail. In some churches communion is served to the congregation in the pews. The kneeling rail is often used for individual counselling and prayer as a response to the sermon or the worship service.

■ ledger strip

a strip of lumber nailed along the bottom of the side of a girder on which joists rest.

■ let-in brace

nominal 1 inch-thick boards applied into notched studs diagonally.

■ level

perfectly horizontal

■ levelling rod

a rod with graduated marks for measuring heights or vertical distances between given points and the line of sight of a levelling instrument. They are longer than a yardstick and are held by a surveyor in a vertical position.

lias

greyish rock which splits easily into slabs.

lierne

a minor rib in a complex rib vault. Liernes do not spring from the main springers. Other types of ribs diagonal, ridge, tierceron, transverse. See **rib vault, springer.**

lierne ribs

vaulting ribs of purely decorative purpose, typical of the Decorated and Perpendicular periods.

lierne vault

a vault including lierne ribs.

life cycle assessment

life cycle assessment is a process to evaluate the environmental burdens associated with a product, process, or activity by identifying and quantifying energy and materials used and wastes released to the environment, assess the impact of those energy and materials used and releases to the environment; and identify and evaluate opportunities to affect environmental improvements. The assessment includes the entire life cycle of the product, process or activity, encompassing, extracting and processing raw materials; manufacturing, transportation and distribution; use, re-use, maintenance; recycling, and final disposal.

life cycle energy

the total energy consumed by a building during its life-cycle (including manufacture of materials, construction, in-use, renovation, and demolition) derived from non-renewable resources. It includes the embodied energy of the building components. Life-cycle energy is usually expressed in terms of source energy that is, the energy content of the primary fuel before generation, distribution and other losses.

light

1. glazing; component part of window, divided by mullions and transoms.
2. space in a window sash for a single pane of glass. Also, a pane of glass.

light shelf

a horizontal element below a window that reflects direct sunlight up onto a ceiling surface.

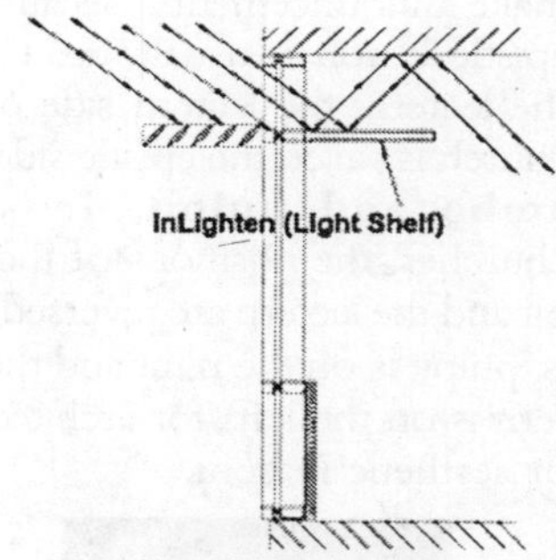

lightening rod

a metal rod that is connected to ground that prevents lightening from damaging a building. Invented by Benjamin Franklin.

limestone

a rock that is formed by the accumulation of organic remains such as shells and coral.

linear

a structure is said to behave linearly when its the deformation response is directly proportional to the loading (i.e. doubling the load doubles the displacement response). For a material, linear means that the stress is directly proportional to the strain.

linear elastic

a force-displacement relationship which is both linear and elastic. For a structure, this means the deformation is proportional to the loading, and deformations disappear on unloading. For a material, the concept is the same except strain substitutes for deformation, and stress substitutes for load.

linenfold

decorative motif in the form of a folded piece of linen cloth. usually carved in low relief.

lining

the covering of internal walls and ceilings of a building. Timber linings include sawn and profiled solid timber, plywood, medium density fibre and other materials.

lintel

1. see **post and lintel.**
2. horizontal stone or beam bridging an opening.
3. a flat horizontal beam which spans the space between two supports.
4. the horizontal structural beam, spanning a door window, or space between columns that supports the structure above it.
5. the top support above an opening such as a window. Lintels support the weight (load) of the building above an opening.
6. a beam of any material used to span an opening.

liquated damages

a monetary amount agreed upon by two parties to a contract prior to performance under the contract that specifies what a either party owes the other if that party defaults under the contract.

liquid-applied membrane

generally applied to cast-in-place concrete surfaces in one or more coats to provide fully-adhered waterproof membranes which conform to all contours.

lite

term for a pane of glass. Also spelled 'light' in industry literature.

live load

1. the total variable weight on a structure. It includes the weights of people, furnishings, snow, wind and earthquake.
2. loads produced by use and occupancy of the building or other structure and do not include construction or environmental loads such as wind load, snow load, ice

load, rain load, seismic load, or dead load.

■ load

an external force. The term load is sometimes used to describe more general actions such as temperature differentials or movements such as foundation settlements.

■ logeion

Greek stage; (pulpitum in the Roman theatre); literally 'a speaking-place'; performances in Hellenistic period included actors placed on a raised platform or stage behind the orchestra and in front of the skene; the roof of the proskenion could be employed for this purpose.

■ loggia

1. a rostrum developed in medieval Italian towns, roofed, slightly elevated, and open on three sides, from which orators could address crowds.

2. an exterior gallery, open on one or more sides, with a colonnade or an arcade. longitudinal barrel vault a barrel (or tunnel) vault which follows the main longitudinal direction of the nave. Usually when a vault is referred to simply as a barrel (or tunnel) vault, it may be assumed to be a longitudinal barrel vault. See **barrel vault, groin vault.**

■ longitudinal

generally parallel to the direction of the wood fibres.

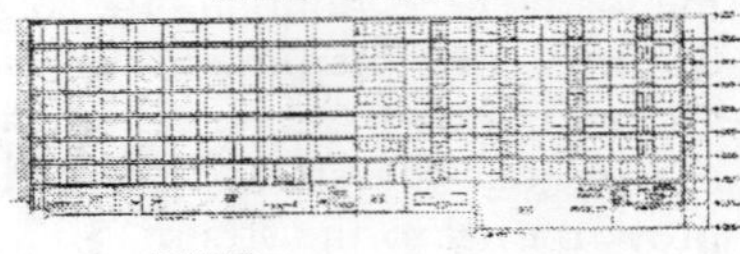

■ longitudinal ridge rib or ridge rib

a rib which runs down the apex of the vault in a longitudinal direction. other types of ribs diagonal, lierne, tierceron, transverse. See **rib vault.**

■ lookout

a short wood bracket or cantilever to support an overhang portion of a roof or the like, usually concealed from view.

■ loop

a narrow opening for the discharge of missiles or arrows.

■ loophole

narrow, tall opening, wallslit for light, air, or shooting through.

■ loose assembled

the fabrication of timber elements off site so that they are finished but not connected together until on site just prior to installation.

■ **loose laid**

in roofing, a membrane 'laid loosely', i.e., not adhered, over a roof deck or Burm.

■ **LOSP**

Light Organic Solvent Preservative. A wood preservative.

■ **lot**

a parcel of ground with boundaries determined by the county.

■ **louver**

1. an opening with a series of horizontal slats so an ranged as to permit ventilation but to exclude rain, sun. light, or vision.
2. opening in roof (sometimes topped with lantern) to allow smoke to escape from central hearth.
3. an opening in roof (often with lantern over) to allow smoke to escape from central hearth.

■ **lozenge**

a diamond shape.

■ **lumber**

the product of the sawmill and planing mill not further manufactured other than by sawing, resawing, and passing lengthwise through a standard planing machine, crosscutting to length, and matching.

■ **lunette**

a semicircular opening (with the flat side down) in a wall over a door, a niche, or a window.

■ **LVL**

see **Laminated Veneer Lumber.**

■ **lyctid borer**

a wood borer, sometimes known as the powder post borer, that can attack some hardwoods.

■ **lyctid susceptibility**

timber is classified according to its susceptibility to attack by lyctid borer.

■ **macellum**

a market structure furnishing meats and poultry and other provisions.

■ **machicolation**

a gallery projecting on brackets and built on the outside of castle towers and walls, with openings in the floor through which to drop molten lead, boiling oil, and missiles. Compare with hoarding.

■ **machicolations**

projecting gallery on brackets, on outside of castle or towers, with holes in floor for dropping rocks, shooting, etc.

maenad

1. a frenzied female follower of Dionysos.
2. the person who physically created an item (as distinct from the person who designed the subject depicted, e.g., the architect.)

mandorla

an almond-shaped motif in which Christ sits; sometimes used also for the Virgin.

mannerism

a prevalent style of art during the later half of the sixteenth century, characterised by a self-aware perspective with dominant, often disturbing, themes or moods. With roots in earlier artistic schools, Mannerist painters often projected themselves as opposition to the idealistic artists of the high Renaissance.

mansard roof

1. a roof having a slope in two planes, the lower of which is usually much steeper. Named after French architect Francois Mansart.
2. a hipped roof with double slopes on all four sides, frequently with the lower slope being steeper than the upper slope. The lower slope is frequently punctuated by the use of dormers.
3. a roof which rises by inclined planes from all four sides of a building. The sloping roofs on all four sides have two pitches, the lower pitch usually very steep and the upper pitch less steep.

mantel

1. the shelf above a fireplace. Also used in referring to the decorative trim around a fireplace opening.
2. detached fortification preventing direct access to a gateway; low outer wall.

marble

a kind of crystallised limestone that can be highly polished.

Photo Galaxy Vol.2 - Photo Textures

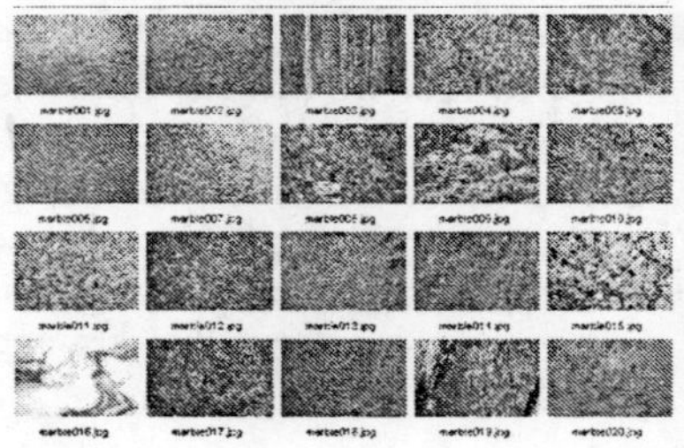

market, marketplace

in ancient Roman cities, the public market was located on or adjacent to the forum and varied somewhat in shape. See **Trajan's market, and the market in Pompeii.**

■ **marquetry**

decorative inlay and veneer work.

■ **mask head**

an animal head employed in conjunction with interlace or foliage motifs.

■ **masonry**

1. construction of brick, stone, adobe, concrete block, or other material set in mortar.
2. stone, brick, concrete, hollow-tile, concrete block, gypsum block, or other similar building units or materials or a combination of the same, bonded together with mortar to form a wall, pier, buttress, or similar mass.

■ **mason's hammer/ Bricklayer's Hammer**

fool shaped like a chisel to trim brick or stone.

■ **mastic**

1. heavy-consistency compound that may remain adhesive and pliable with age. Is typically a waterproof compound applied to exterior walls and roof surfaces.
2. a pasty material used as a cement (as for setting tile) or a protective coating (as for thermal insulation or waterproofing.)

■ **matched lumber**

lumber that is dressed and shaped on one edge in a grooved pattern and on the other in a tongued pattern.

■ **mausoleum**

1. structure for a tomb. Compare with sarcophagus, memorial brass.
2. mausoleum comes from the Greek word 'mausoleion', meaning a large tomb.

■ **maximum occupancy load**

the maximum number of people permitted in a room and is measured per foot for each width of exit door. The maximum is 50 per foot of exit.

■ **meander or Greek key**

an ornamental motif consisting of continuous bands arranged in rectilinear forms.

mechanically laminated timber

laminated timber where the laminations are joined with mechanical fasteners.

medallions

an ornamental relief uses on wall or ceilings as decoration. Often, medallions will carry information such as a building name or construction date.

media cavea

Latin: middle section of auditorium seating. Roman middle tier of cavea seating

Medium Density Fibreboard (MDF)

a panel product manufactured from lignocelluloses fibres combined with a synthetic resin or other suitable binder.

membrane

a generic term relating to a variety of sheet goods used for certain built-up roofing repairs and application.

memorial brass

an engraved metal plate used as a commemorative monument. Sometimes these were set vertically, usually in a wall, but usually they were set horizontally, flush with the pavement of a church, to mark a tomb. The engraved areas were often filled with pigment. Compare with mausoleum, sarcophagus

merlon

the high segment of the alternating high and low segments of a battlement.

meta

the points where chariots turned in races in a Roman circus (such as the Circus Maximus). The first turn was called the meta prima, the second the meta secunda.

metal edge

brake metal or metal extrusions which are secured at the perimeter of the roof to form a weather-tight seal.

metal lath

sheets of metal that are slit and drawn out to form openings. Used as a plaster base for walls and ceilings and as reinforcing over other forms of plaster base.

meter

electric resistance moisture - a meter that measures the electrical resistance of timber, which is converted to a reading of timber moisture content. They are usually calibrated for Douglas Fir. The reading must then be corrected for temperature and species. Capacitance Moisture - a meter that measures the varying capacitance of wood with changing moisture content using a radio frequency oscillator. They measure the amount of water per unit volume in the wood.

metope

the square space between triglyphs in a doric frieze.

meurtriere

an opening in the roof of a passage where soldiers could shoot into the room below. Also see **'Murder Holes'.**

■ **meutrieres**

murder holes.

■ **meze or mezedes**

appetisers.

■ **mezzanine**

low storey introduced between two loftier ones, usually the ground and first floors.

■ **micro-hydropower**

micro-hydropower is similar to hydropower, except it can be achieved through the use of a small stream.

■ **migration**

spreading or creeping of a constituent of a compound onto/ into adjacent surfaces. See **bleeding.**

■ **mil thickness**

measurement used to determine thickness of a coating. 1 mil = .001 inch (1/1000).

■ **mildew**

a fungal growth that does not cause deep discoloration of the wood. Associated with mould, it usually appears as tiny black spots that cover the timber surface.

■ **mill**

a building or site that accommodates a manufacturing process Green - a site for sawing, packing and racking unseasoned timber. Dry - a site for processing and storing seasoned timber.

■ **millwork**

generally all building materials made of finished wood and manufactured in millwork plants and planing mills are included under the term 'millwork.' It includes such items as inside and outside doors, window and doorframes, blinds, porch work, mantels, panel work, stairways, moldings, and interior trim. It normally does not include flooring, ceiling, or siding.

■ **minaret**

a slender, lofty tower with balconies attached to a Muslim mosque.

■ **mineral spirits**

a by-product of petroleum, clear in colour, a solvent for asphalt coatings.

■ **minoan period**

this period (3000 - 1100 BC.) is named after the great Minoan civilisation on Crete. Influenced by the Mesopotamians and Egyptians, the Minoans were a maritime power that had their own script similar to Egyptian hieroglyphics and later a script called Linear A that has not been translated. Their pottery, metalwork, and cities are well preserved but it is theorised the civilisation declined after an enormous volcanic eruption on Santorini. The period is divided into early (3000 - 2100 BC.), middle (2100 - 1500 BC.), and late (1500 - 1100 BC.) phases.

■ **minster**

originally the church of a monastery, then became used to describe any large church. Best known example, York Minster.

■ **misericord**

a bracket on the underside of a hinged wooden seat in a choir stall providing support during standing. Often richly carved.

■ **mission revival**

popular style from the 1890s through the 1930s. Characteristics include curvilinear parapets, stucco finish, semi-circular arches, tile roof, bell towers and other features.

■ **miter joint**

the joint of two pieces at an angle that bisects the joining angle. For example, the miter joint at the side and head casing at a door opening is made at a 45° angle.

■ **moat**

a ditch, usually filled with water, surrounding a castle. A common first line of defence.

■ **mock-up testing**

controlled air, water and structural performance testing of existing or new glazing systems.

■ **modillion**

a sort of decorative bracket supporting the cornice, normally with a double scroll motif.

■ **modillions**

small brackets, usually in pairs, which supports the cornice of the corinthian and composite orders.

■ **module**

the measurement that architects use to determine the proportions of a structure, for example, the diameter of a column.

■ **modulus**

stress at a given strain. Also tensile strength at a given elongation.

■ **modulus of elasticity**

the proportional constant between stress and strain for material with linear elastic behaviour calculated as stress divided by strain. Modulus of elasticity can be interpreted as the slope of the stress-strain graph. It is usually denoted as E, sometimes known as Young's Modulus Y, or E-Modulus.

■ **moisture content**

the weight of moisture contained in a piece of timber expressed as a percentage of the oven dry weight.

■ **moisture content class**

classification of timber by moisture content. Green, Green off Saw —Freshly sawn timber or timber that has received essentially no formal drying. Air Dried - timber that has been air or shed dried to an average of 25% moisture content or lower, with no material having more than 30% moisture content. Pre-dried - timber that has been air dried or dried in a predryer to FSP. Kiln Dried - timber dried in a kiln or by some other refined method, to an average specified moisture content, typically 8% to 14%, or to a moisture content understood to be suitable for a certain application.

■ **moisture content of wood**

weight of the water contained in the wood, usually expressed as a percentage of the weight of the ovendry wood.

■ **moisture gradient**

a progressive decrease (or increase) in moisture content between the core and the surface of a piece of wood.

■ **moisture movement**

the transfer of moisture from one point to another within wood or other materials.

■ **molding**

1. in architecture, a continuous, narrow surface (projecting or recesses, plain or ornamented) designed to break up a surface, to accent, or to decorate.
2. a wood strip having a coned or projecting surface used for decorative purposes, e.g., door and window trim.

■ **moline**

ends curling outward.

■ **moment**

the resultant of a system of forces causing rotation without translation. A moment can be expressed as a couple.

■ **moment of inertia**

a property of a two dimensional cross section shape with respect to an axis, usually an axis through the centroid of the shape.

■ **moment release**

see **pin connection.**

■ **moment resisting-connection**

see **fixed connection.**

■ **monastery**

a self contained, organised religious community, and the communal buildings around which the life of the inhabitants revolves.

■ **moni**

monastery.

■ **monitor**

a large structure rising above the surrounding roof planes, designed to give light and/or ventilation to the building interior.

■ **monstrance**

container for eucharistic wafers which contains an opening through which they can be viewed.

■ **mopping**

in roofing, a layer of hot bitumen mopped between plies of roofing felt. Full mopping is the application of bitumen by mopping in such a manner that the surface being mopped is entirely coated with a reasonably uniform coating. Spot Mopping is the procedure of applying hot bitumen in a random fashion of small daubs, as compared to full mopping. Sprinkle mopping is a special application of installing insulation to the decks. It is done by dipping a roof mop into hot bitumen and sprinkling the material onto the deck. Strip Mopping is the application of bitumen in parallel bands.

■ mortal

someone who is subject to death.

■ mortar

a mixture of sand, water, and lime used to bind stones together; as opposed to dry laid masonry.

■ mortar types

type M is suitable for general use and is recommended specifically for masonry below grade and in contact with earth, such as foundations, retaining walls and walks. Type M is the strongest type. Type S is suitable for general use and is recommended where high resistance to lateral forces is required. Type N is suitable for general use in exposed masonry above grade and is recommended specifically for exterior walls subject to severe exposures. Type 0 is recommended for load-bearing walls of solid units where the compressive stresses do not exceed 100 lbs. per square inch and the masonry wall not be subjected to freezing and thawing in the presence of excessive moisture.

■ mortice and tenon joint

a joint where a hole or slot known as a mortice (a) is formed in a piece of timber to receive the reduced end of similar size or tenon (b) from another piece. The joint is often secured with wedges, dowels or steel plates.

■ mortise

a slot cut into a board, plank, or timber, usually edgewise, to receive tenon of another board, plank, or timber to form a joint.

■ mosaic

a decoration created by setting small pieces of glass, stone, or marble in a matrix- often concrete. Wall mosaics were most prevalent in the Early Christian and Byzantine periods, during which they were a very important form of wall decoration.

■ motte

a high mound of earth on which a lord's residence is placed usually during the eleventh-and-twelfth-century castles.

■ **motte-&-bailey**

1. earth mound with wood or stone keep, surrounded by ditched and palisaded enclosure (or courtyard.)
2. a defensive system consisting of a mound of earth (the motte) with a wooden tower on top, placed within a courtyard (the bailey, also called the ward). Compare with keep.

■ **motte-and-bailey castle**

an early form of castle with a wooden or stone keep.

■ **mould**

a fungal growth on timber or other wood products at or near the surface and, therefore, not typically resulting in deep discoloration. Mould is usually ash green to deep green, although black and yellow are also common. See **mildew.**

■ **moulding**

the profile given to a projection on a building such as a string course. There are any number of profiles most of which are self explanatory. Best known are Bird's beak; Bead and reel; Cable, (like a rope); Cavetto, (a moulding with a concave profile describing a quater of a circle); Chevron; Cyma recta, (convex to concave); Cyma reversa, or ogee, (concave to convex); Egg and dart (eggs and arrow heads, representing life and death); Dogtooth; Nailhead (small projections resembling nail heads); Ovolo (egg-shaped) etc.

■ **movement**

the extent of expansion and contraction which occurs with dried wood as its moisture content responds to changes in relative humidity in service.

■ **mud cracks**

cracks developing from the normal shrinkage of an emulsion coating when applied too heavily.

■ **mullion**

1. vertical division of windows.
2. the vertical element that separates the lancets of a window.
3. a vertical member that divides a window or that separates one window from another.
4. a vertical bar or divider in the frame between windows, doors, or other openings that supports and holds such items as panels, glass, sash, or sections of a curtain wall.

■ **mullions**

1. a member that supports and separates windows or doors.
2. the supporting pieces in a glazed window, typically made of wood, steel or aluminium.

■ **muntins**

1. wood bars used to hold glass panes in divided light windows.
2. horizontal or vertical bars that divide the sash frame into smaller

lights of glass. Muntins are smaller in dimensions and weight than mullions.

mural

wall (adjectival).

murder holes

a section between the main gate and a inner portcullis where arrows, rocks, and hot oil can be dropped from the roof though holes. Provides good cover for defenders and leaves the attacker open. Only used when outer gate has been breach.

mycenaean period

the decline of the Minoans led to the rise of the Mycenaeans from 1900 - 1100 BCE. Their independent city-states in the Peloponnese were characterised by palaces on fortified hilltops, they wrote in the deciphered Linear B script, and many fine examples of their gold jewellery are on display at the National Archaeological Museum in Athens. Also called Achaeans, the height of their civilisation was in 1300 BCE. but was in decline by 1100 BCE. with the arrival of the Dorians.

nail

a sharpened piece of metal or plastic driven into timber to fasten a joint.

nail gun

a hand-operated tool powered by compressed air which drives nails.

nail laminated timber

a built up product made of layers of laminations of wood, all with the grain laid parallel and nailed together.

nail plate connector

sheet metal plates stamped so that nails are formed on one side and pressed into timber to make a joint.

nail plate truss

a truss where the node joints are joined with nail plates.

nail ring

a generally rectangular pattern of nails used to join timber elements.

nailer

a piece of lumber secured to non-nailable decks and walls by bolts or other means, which provides a suitable backing onto which roof components may be mechanically fastened.

nailhead

1. pyramid moulding.
2. an ornamental motif of small pyramids, said to represent the heads of nails. Very popular in the 12th century.

nanecropolisrthex

1. the historic term for what might otherwise be called the foyer or entry way of the church.
2. an enclosed passage from the nave to the main entrance of a church.
3. a low projection at the western end of a church, like a porch. Although narthex is sometimes used synonymously with west work, a narthex is usually more open and often has only one story in contrast to the more closed west work

with a large open chamber on the upper level. Compare with west work, screen facade. See **west end.**
4. a porch or vestibule of a church, generally colonnaded or arcaded and preceding the nave.

natatio

the swimming pool in a Roman bath complex.

natural

salt crystallisation, where salts within the stone are drawn to the surface by the process of wetting and drying, where they crystallise can be very damaging. If the pore structure of the stone is unable to accommodate the resulting expansion, the surface of the stone can disintegrate. Frost action is probably the next most damaging occurrence, followed by the action of organisms such as algaes and lichens and plants such as ivy. Air pollutants, are no longer such a problem following the clean air acts.

natural finish

a transparent finish which does not seriously alter the original colour or grain of the natural wood. Natural finishes are usually provided by sealers, oils, varnishes, water-repellent preservatives, and other similar materials.

nave

1. the architectural term for the place where the congregation gathers for worship, as opposed to the front part of the church from which the service is lead. In churches with a lecture-hall floor plan, the term 'sanctuary' is often used to mean both chancel and nave because the two are not architecturally distinct. An oratory is a room or a portion of a room that is set aside for an individual to conduct personal devotions. The word oratory comes from a Latin word that means a place to pray.
2. principal hall of a church, extending from the narthex to the chancel.
3. the principal area of a church, extending from the main area to the transept.
4. the central longitudinal space of a bascilican church. It is usually flanked on its lond sides by aislas which are separated from the nave by columns or piers. In many churches, the lay congregation stand in the nave to attend religious services. Other parts of a church ambulatory, apse, choir, crossing, east end, choir, transept, west end.
5. the part of a church between the chief entrance and the choir (quire), demarcated from aisles by piers or columns.

neat plaster

a base coat plaster which does not contain aggregates and is used where the addition of aggregates on the job is desired.

■ **necking**

ornament at the top of a column, bottom of the capital.

■ **necropolis**

an ancient cemetery.

■ **neoclassical**

also frequently referred to as Classical Revival. Ancient Roman and Greek architecture inspired Neoclassical style architecture. The style can be described as monumental, utilising columns, pediments and sparing ornamentation. The style is most frequently found in public buildings and mansions.

■ **Neolithic period**

the period from 7000 - 3000 BC. affected mainly the central landmass of Greece in the region known as Thessaly. The people grew crops and raised animals and by 3000 BC. they were living in settlements with streets and houses. The most complete Neolithic settlements in Greece are found near the modern day city of Volos.

■ **neoprene**

a synthetic rubber having physical properties closely resembling those of natural rubber. It is made by polymerising chloroprene, and the latter is produced from acetylene and hydrogen chloride.

■ **net vault**

a vault on which a complex of ribs gives a net-like appearance. See **rib vault.** Other types of rib vaults fan vault, quadripartite rib vault, sexpartite rib vault.

■ **newel**

1. centre post of spiral staircase.
2. a post to which the end of a stair railing or balustrade is fastened. Also, any post to which a railing or balustrade is fastened.

■ **niche**

a recess in the thickness of a wall.

■ **nogging**

a short horizontal timber strut fixed between studs or joists in framed construction to provide lateral stiffening and intermediate fixing points for cladding or lining.

■ **nonbearing wall**

a wall supporting no load other than its own weight.

non-destructive

a phrase describing a method of examining the interior of a component whereby no damage is done to the component itself.

non-drying (non-curing)

a sealant that does not set up or cure. See **butyl.**

non-sag

a sealant formulation having a consistency that will permit application in vertical joints without appreciable sagging or slumping. A performance characteristic which allows the sealant to be installed in a sloped or vertical joint application without appreciable sagging or slumping.

non-skinning

descriptive of a product that does not form a surface skin.

non-staining

characteristic of a compound that will not stain a surface.

nook-shaft

shaft set in angle of jamb or pier.

normal strain

strain measuring the intensity of deformation along an axis. Normal strain is usually denoted by average normal strain between two points is calculated as where L is the original distance between the points, and is the change in that distance. Normal strain is often simply called strain.

normal stress

stress acting perpendicular to an imaginary plane cutting through an object. Normal stress has two senses compression and tension. Normal stress is often simply called stress.

Norman

a style of buildings erected by the Normans (1066 - 1154) based on the Italian Romanesque. It was used principally in castles, churches, and abbeys of massive proportions. Sparsely decorated masonry and the use of the round arch are characteristic.

nosing

the rounded front edge of a stair tread that extends over the riser.

notch

a crosswise rabbet at the end of a board.

nozzle

the tubular tip of a caulking gun through which the compound is extruded.

nuclear meter

a device used to detect moisture by measuring slowed, deflected neutrons.

nymphaeum

a rocky outcrop or fountain house, either natural or artificially made, which supplies water. The sites were dedicated to the Nymphs.

O. G. (or ogee)

a molding with a profile in the form of a letter S; having the outline of a reversed curve. A molding with a profile in the form of a letter S; having the outline of a reversed curve.

■ O.C.

'On Centre'. A measurement term meaning a certain distance between like materials. Studs rafters, joists, and the like in a building placed at 16 inches O.C. will be laid out so that there is 16 inches from the centre of one stud to the centre of the next.

■ o'lite

granular limestone.

■ oculus

circular opening in a roof or on a wall, such as the oculus in the centre of the dome of the Pantheon.

■ oculus

a circular or eye shaped window.

■ odeion

a small theatre, often roofed, used for smaller entertainment venues such as performed music or poetry readings.

■ odeion/odeon

ancient Greek small theatre roofed off from the sky, unlike theatres which were open air.

■ odos

street.

■ oecus

the living room of a Roman house (domus). Sometimes used as a dining room or for entertaining.

■ offset

ledge marking the narrowing of a wall's thickness.

■ ogee

a pointed arch with double curved sides, upper arcs convex, lower concave.

■ ogee or ogive arch

an arch with a pointed apex, formed by the intersection of two S curves usually confined to decoration and not used in arcade arches. Ogee arches were used only in the late Gothic period. other types of arches: depressed, horseshoe

■ oil-canning

the term describing distortion of thin-gauge metal panels which are fastened in a manner restricting normal thermal movement.

■ **oilette**

a round opening at the base of a loophole, usually for a cannon muzzle.

■ **omphalos**

a stone at Delfi that Greeks believed marked the centre of the world.

■ **oolite**

granular limestone.

■ **open grained**

common classification for woods with large pores in the grain. Also known as coarse textured.

■ **open joint**

wide space between faces of stones.

■ **open web truss**

a truss where the webs are open and visible.

■ **opisthodomos**

also called Posticum, a small room in the Cella of a Classical temple used as a treasury.

■ **oracle**

sacred place where ancient Greeks could ask their gods, through a priestess, to give them advise or to foretell the future. The most famous oracle was that of Apollo at Delphi.

■ **orant (orans) figure**

a standing figure with both arms raised. This was a gesture of p-rayer in the Early Christian period.

■ **oratory**

a small private chapel usually in a house.

■ **orcheomai**

see **orchestra.**

■ **orchestra**

literally 'the dancing floor or place,' from the Greek 'orche-omai' - circular in early Greek theatre construction, semi-circular in Roman constructions, the orchestra was the space between the audience and the stage; primary chorus performance space in Greco-Roman theatre; also adapted for use as an arena for Roman 'spectacle entertainment'.

■ **order**

a term applied to the three styles of Greek architecture, the Dorian, Corinthian, and Ionic, referring to the style of columns and their entablatures; it also refers to the Composite and the Tuscan, developed from the original three orders.

■ **organic building materials**

these materials are those based on carbon compounds. They include sawn timber, reconstituted and engineered wood products and plastics.

■ **oriel**

projecting window in wall; originally a form of porch, usually of wood; side-turret.

■ **orillons**

arrowhead bastions.

■ **orthogonal**

characterised by straight lines in parallel and perpendicular arrangements. 'Lines' may be walls, rows of columns, or axis lines. See **Plan**

of San Lorenzo, Florence, Italy.

■ Ottoman period

for nearly 400 years (1453 - 1829 A.D.) the Ottoman Empire controlled Greece although they continually struggled with Venice for control. In the beginning, the Greeks preferred the rule of the Ottomans to the Venetians who were ruthless subjugators but eventually they resented the rule of the Ottomans as well. It was in 1627 during a battle with the Venetians that a shell struck a gunpowder store on the Acropolis in Athens and blew it up. In the late 1700's the Russians came to Greece in an effort to expand their power base. On March 25, 1821 the Greeks began their War of Independence and the Ottoman Empire finally fell in 1829.

■ Ottonian art

a German art form which preceded the Romanesque, and followed the Carolingian, in which can be seen some early beginnings of forms and innovations what would later be fundamental to Gothic structures. A primary feature of some Ottonian churches was the use of systematic pier and column support within the Nave.

■ oubliette

a dungeon reached by a trap door; starvation hole.

■ outer curtain

the wall the encloses the outer ward.

■ outer ward

the area around the outside of and adjacent to the inner curtain.

■ outhouse

a small structure used as a toilet and always built away from the main living quarters.

■ outrigger

a support beam that extends beyond the wall of a building at the ridgeline used to support a hoist.

■ oven dry

a term used to describe wood that has been dried in a ventilated oven at 102 C to 105 C until there is no additional loss in weight. Weight - The weight of wood when all the water has been driven off by heating the wood in an oven.

■ overcut

an allowance added to the nominal dimension of an unseasoned board to compensate for shrinkage during drying.

■ overhang

the end of timber that is unsupported by rack sticks and extends beyond the ends of most pieces in an air drying stack, rack, pack, or unit of timber.

■ pack

a unit of timber boards

■ pagoda

a temple or sacred building, typically in an Asian nation, usually pyramidal, forming a tower with upward curving roofs over the individual stories.

paint

a combination of pigments with suitable thinners or oils to provide decorative and protective coatings.

palace

1. the official residence of a sovereign.
2. the domestic building for Roman emperors, at the scale of a small city.

In Diocletian's palace in Split or Spalato, Yugoslavia, the form is based on a Roman 'castrum' or camp, i.e., it is square in plan and divided into four quadrants. Unlike the castrum, it was solidly built and employed sumptuous materials. It was 300 by 400 meters square or 984' x 1312'.

palaestra

(or Palestra) A large square or rectangular space, open to the air, surrounded by porticos held up by rows of columns. Such structures were used for athletic training and wrestling. At times associated with Roman Bath complexes. Originally a Greek building type.

palaistra

purpose designed building, smaller than a gymnasium, with dressing rooms and a sand covered courtyard where Greek boys were taught athletics and wrestling.

palisade

1. a wooden defensive fence.
2. a sturdy wooden fence usually built to enclose a site until a permanent stone wall can be constructed.

palladian window

a large arched window with divided lights, bordered by two smaller, but proportional, rectangular windows with divided lights.

palladium

according to the myth, when the goddess Athena was still a young girl, she was brought up in the house of the god Triton whose daughter, Pallas, was as equally talented as Athena in the art of war. During a fight between the two girls, Athena killed Pallas by accident in front of Zeus. The goddess, suffering the loss of her friend, used her considerable technical ability to build the famous Palladium (a wooden statue) in the likeness of her friend. She put it under her aegis (armour plate) and described its divine honours. In art it is normally noted as a statuette depicting the goddess Athena.

palmette

looped like a palm-leaf.

panel

in house construction, a thin flat piece of wood, ply. wood, or similar material, framed by stiles and rails as in a door or fitted into grooves of thicker material with molded edges for decorative wall treatment.

pantheon

a temple to all the gods.

parabolic arch

an arch whose curve is a parabola.

parados

low wall in inner side of main wall.

parapet

a low wall on the outer side of the main wall, protecting the front of the entry walk.

parapet wall

a low wall around the perimeter of a roof deck.

paraskenion

(pl. paraskenion) - Hellenistic: projecting side additions to the skene; one to two story side wings on either side of the proskenion; could be ornamented with columns or pillars supporting a frieze; equivalent to Roman versurae.

parge coat

a thin application of plaster for coating a wall.

parking strip

the area in front of a building between the sidewalk and the street usually landscaped with grass. The parking strip serves as a buffer between the road and pedestrians walking on the sidewalk.

parodos

(pl. parodoi) one of the side entrances into the orchestra of a Greek theatre; the space between the auditorium wall and the skene building; primary entrance/exit for the chorus; also the song sung by chorus as it first enters the orchestra.

parquetry flooring

flooring of small matching pieces of timber laid on a substrate in a geometric patterns.

particle board

a pressed sheet material made from particles of timber or other ligno-cellulosic material bonded with synthetic resin and/or other organic binder.

parting stop or strip

a small wood piece used in the side and head jambs of double-hung windows to separate upper and lower sash.

partition

a wall that subdivides spaces within any story of a building.

parts of an arch

keystone, soffit, spring line, springer, voussoir. Measurements of an archrise, span. Related architectural elements arcade, cusp, hood moulding, spandrel, tympanum. See **intersecting arch, blind arch, relieving arch, Shapes of arches.**

party wall

a wall between two adjoining living quarters in a multi-family dwelling.

passive solar

passive solar is the technology of heating and cooling a building naturally, through the use of energy efficient materials, and proper site placement of the structure.

paten

a plate on which the eucharistic wafer was placed. See **chalice, ciborium, monstrance, pyx.**

patina

a surface change due to age or use, such as the fine oxidation of copper or the weathering of wood.

patterned glass

on type of rolled glass having a pattern impressed on one or both sides. Used extensively for light control, bath enclosures and decorative glazing. Sometimes call 'rolled,' 'figured,' or 'obscure' glass.

paver stones

usually pre-cast concrete slabs used to create a traffic surface.

PEC

Pigmented Emulsified Creosote, a wood preservative.

pedagogies

domestic slaves with particular responsibility for accompanying Greek boys to school.

pediment

1. in a classical-style building, the triangular segment between the horizontal entablature and the sloping roof.
2. a triangular space above a window or entrance. Originally the triangular space was formed by the end of a gable roof and later was used decoratively Contrast with tympanum.
3. in classical architecture, the low-pitched gable above the entablature, usually filled with sculpture.

peel

a small tower; typically, a fortified house on the border.

pellet

circular boss.

pen flourished initial

an ornamental initial charact-erised by abstract, rhythmic patterns, usually drawn in red or blue ink. Pen flourished initials were especially common during the twelfth and thirteenth centuries. See **illuminated initial.** Compare with other types of illuminated initial.

pendant

a hanging architectural member formed by ribs. Not to be confused with pendentive. Pendants of the appear in conjunction with fan vaults. See **fan vault**.

pendentive

a curved support shaped like an inverted triangle, used to support a dome.

pendular vault

complex vault of the perpendicular period, typified by pendulous carved features. Oxford Cathedral has one in the Choir.

penny

as applied to nails, it originally indicated the price per hundred. The term now series as a measure of nail length and is abbreviated by the letter d.

penthouse

a relatively small structure built above the plane of the roof.

peplos

long garment made from a rectangle of cloth draped around the body and pinned at the shoulders, with a mantle draped over the shoulders.

performance and payment bond

guaranty by a surety company that if a contractor fails to perform under a contract, the surety company will complete the work.

performance based

a code where the requirements are expressed as objectives to be achieved

peribolos

enclosed court surrounding a temple.

peripteral

a term describing a monument surrounded by a single row of columns.

periptero

a street kiosk. They are found in every city in Greece and sell everything from candy bars to stamps.

peristyle

a court or garden (as at Pompeii) surrounded by porticos with columns.

peristyle

columns surrounding a building or enclosing a courtyard.

perlite

an aggregate formed by heating and expanding siliceous volcanic glass.

perm

a measure of water vapour movement through a material (grains per square foot per hour per inch of mercury difference in vapour pressure.)

permanent set

a change in the properties of wood which can occur during drying when stressing exceeds the elastic limit. Permanent set prevents normal shrinkage of the timber and can lead to more obvious defects such as casehardening and honeycombing.

permeability

the ease with which a fluid flows through a porous material (wood) in response to pressure.

perpendicular

1. english architectural style (1330-1540).
2. of or relating to a style of English Gothic architecture of the 14th and 15th centuries, characterised by emphasis of the vertical element.
3. the final English Gothic style, typified by large windows and tall, slender pillars. The choir of Gloucester is a good example.

petit appareil

small cubical stonework.

pew

originally, Christians stood for worship, and that is still the case in many eastern churches. The pew, a long, backed bench upon which congregants sit, was an innovation of western medieval Christianity. Pews were inherited by Protestants from the Roman Catholic Church, and because of their practicality, have spread to some orthodox churches located in the west.

piazza, plaza or urban space

'piazza' is the Italian word for a large open space in a city created or defined by several buildings forming a perimeter enclosure. In English speaking countries this space is called a 'plaza' or an 'urban space.'

pier

1. a column or post supporting a superstructure such as floor bearers, beams, etc., or an internal support for a bridge.
2. an upright support, generally square, rectangular, or composite. In medieval architecture there are massive circular supports called drum piers. Compare with column, pilaster, types of pier compound, drum. See **alternation of support.**
3. a solid vertical supporting member, usually stone, brick, or concrete, square or polygonal in section, and broad in relation to its height.

pigment

a powdered solid in suitable degree of subdivision for use in paint or enamel.

pilaster

1. a true pilaster is a rectangular element of vertical masonry which projects only slightly from the wall and has both a capital and a base Contrast with column, pier Parts of pilasters base, capital, shaft.
2. similar to an engaged column, but a rectangular strip standing out slightly from a wall.
3. flat, rectangular, vertical member projecting from a wall of which it forms a part. Usually has a base and a capital and is often fluted.

pilasters

masonry projection from a building, but usually decorative in nature and not load bearing (however they may be concealing a load bearing member.)

pile

a structural timber driven deep into soil or rock to provide a secure foundation for structures.

pillar

1. 'pillar' means 'a strong vertical support' and is therefore vague. Unless one means 'a monumental column or shaft standing alone' as in 'The Pillars of Hercules', it is best to use the alternative: column, post, pier or pilaster.
2. usually a weight-carrying member, such as a pier or a column; sometimes an isolated, freestanding structure used for commemorative purposes.

piloti

column on an unenclosed ground floor carrying a raised building above.

pin connection

in two dimensions, a pin connection restrains two translation degrees of freedom but does not restrain rotation. Since the rotation degree of freedom is unrestrained at a pin connection, it transfers no moment.

pin joint

a connection free to rotate like a hinge.

pin support

in two dimensions, a pin support restrains two translation degrees of freedom but does not restrain rotation. When considering reaction forces, a pin support is usually considered to have two force components one each about the x and y axes respectively.

pinakes

painted panels; temporary scenic elements usually placed in the openings (thyromata) of the Greek skene

pinnacle

a pointed termination of a spire, buttress, or other extremity of a building. Pinnacles are sometimes ornamented. Compare with spire.

piscina

hand basin with drain, usually set against or into a wall.

pitch

1. roof slope.
2. the incline slope of a roof or the ratio of the total rise to the total width of a house, i.e., an 8-foot rise and 24-foot width is a one-third pitch roof. Roof slope is expressed in the inches of rise per foot of run.
3. a term frequently used to designate coal tar pitch.

pitch pocket

an opening extending parallel to the annual rings of growth, that usually contains, or has contained, either solid or liquid pitch.

pitching

rough cobbling on floor, as in courtyards.

pitching

rough cobbling.

pith

the small soft core occurring in the centre of a tree trunk, branch, twig, or log.

pithos

minoan jars or vases, sometimes taller than a person, that were used for storage.

plain-sawn timber

timber converted so that the growth rings meet the face in any part at an angle of less than 45 degrees. Also called backsawn timber.

plan

the drawing of the horizontal plane of a building, cut through the walls at about three feet above a floor and looking down. Also called a floor plan.

plan submittal

submission of construction plans to the city or county in order to obtain a building permit.

plans

see **blue prints.**

plantation

an intensively managed stand of trees of either native or introduced species, created by the regular placement of seedlings or seed

plaster grounds

strips of wood used as guides or strike off edges around window and door openings and at base of walls.

plastic

see **inelastic**.

plat

1. a map of a geographical area as recorded by the county.
2. a horizontal framing member laid flat.
3. a horizontal member anchored to a masonry wall.
4. bottom horizontal member of a frame wall.
5. top horizontal member of a frame wall supporting ceiling joists, rafters, or other members. 10.

plate glass

a large window that is a single solid sheet of glass.

plate line

the top horizontal line of a building wall upon which the roof rests.

plate tracery

tracery which uses thick areas of stone to separate glozed areas. The window may look as if it had been filled in with stone, then small openings cut through for the glass. The stone rather than the glass dominates the window. Contrast with bar tracery

plateia

square.

platform framing/Platform Construction

a system of framing a building in which floor joists of each story rest on the top plates of the story below or on the foundation sill for the first story, and the bearing walls and partitions rest on the subfloor of each story. (Usually one story constitutes a platform.)

plenum/Plenum Chamber

chamber or container for moving air under a slight positive pressure to which one or more ducts are connected.

plinth

projecting base of wall.

plot plan

a bird's eye view showing how a building sits on the building lot, typically showing setbacks (how far the building must sit from the road), easements, rights of way, and drainage.

plough

to cut a lengthwise groove in a board or plank.

plumb

straight up and down, perfectly vertical.

ply

1. one layer of a laminated sheet.
2 a term to denote the number of thicknesses or layers of roofing felt, veneer in plywood, or layers in built-up materials, in any finished piece of such material.

plywood
an assembled product made up of veneers of timber glued together so that the grain of alternate layers is at right angles.

pocket
a patch of bark or gum (kino) completely or partially enclosed in the wood.

pocket (channel)
a three-sided, U-shaped opening in a sash or frame to receive glazing infill. Contrasted to a rabbet, which is a two-sided, L-shaped sections as with face glazed window sash.

podium
raised platform, shelf, or stage. see **logeion**.

pointing
the process where joints between masonry units, brick, etc., are filled with mortar.

polar coordinates
the system of urban planning employed by the ancient Greeks in determining the placement of buildings in the sacred precinct. This ordering system is based on a single fixed point, usually the propylaea, from which the buildings are placed so that their volume is apparent, and no building is hidden by another.

pole
a round timber column.

polis
the ancient Greek 'city-state', was composed of both rural and urban areas. There was only one city for each polis and the citizens of the polis took their name from the principal god that they worshiped; thus the Athenians worshiped the goddess of wisdom and war, Athena. Map of Athens, 400 BC.

polished wired glass
wired glass that has been ground and polished on both surfaces.

polychromy
multicoloured pigments.

polyethylene glycol
a chemical pretreating agent used to improve the drying behaviour of timber.

polysulphide sealant
polysulphide liquid polymer sealant which is mercaptan terminated, long chain aliphatic polymers containing disulfide linkages. They can be converted to rubbers at room temperature without shrinkage upon addition of a curing agent.

polyurethane sealant
an organic compound formed by reaction of a glycol with and isocyanate.

Polyvinyl Chloride (PVC)
polymer formed by polymerisation of vinyl chloride monomer. Sometimes called vinyl.

pending
a condition where water stands on a roof for prolonged periods due to poor drainage and/or deflection of the deck.

■ **pop rivets**

fasteners used to join pieces of metal that are installed by either compressed-air-assisted or hand-operated guns. Unique in that they are installed from one side of the work.

■ **porch**

entry point to the church, a shelter adjoining a door. Often decorated.

■ **pores**

wood cells of comparatively large diameter that have open ends and are set one above the other to form continuous tubes. The openings of the vessels on the surface of a piece of wood are referred to as pores.

■ **porosity**

the density of substance and its capacity to pass liquids.

■ **porta reggia**

Latin: 'royal door'; central stage entrance in the Roman scaenae.

■ **portae hospitales**

Latin: 'guest doors'; two doors on either side of the central door in the Roman scaenae.

■ **portal**

a planar frame where the lateral and bending forces are transferred by moment resisting connections from the portal rafters to the columns.

■ **portcullis**

a heavy timber or metal grill that protected the castle entrance and could be raised or lowered from within the castle. It dropped vertically between grooves to block passage or barbican, or to trap attackers.

■ **portcullis**

a grating dropped vertically from grooves to block passage or gate in castle; of wood, metal or a combination of the two.

■ **porte cochere**

a structure with a roof that extends from the sides or front entrance of a home over a nearby driveway to shelter those getting in or out of vehicles.

■ **portico**

a structure usually attached to a building, such as a porch, consisting of a roof supported by piers or columns.

■ **porticus**

(stoa) building having its roof supported by one or more rows of columns parallel to the rear wall; often a market building

■ **portland cement**

a mixture of certain minerals which when mixed with water form a grey coloured paste and cure into a very hard mass.

■ **portus post scaenium**

Latin: a portico or passageway behind the scaenae (scene building)of a Roman theatre.

■ **post**

a column or a free standing axially loaded compression member, usually vertical.

■ **post & beam construction**

most common type of wall framing, using posts which carry horizontal beams on which joists are supported. It allows for fewer bearing partitions, & less material.

■ **post and lintel**

a method of construction in which vertical beams (posts) are used to support a horizontal beam (lintel.)

■ **post-and-lintel construction**

a building method that uses two upright or vertical posts set a distance apart with a horizontal beam or lintel placed on top of them to span the distance. Walls and roofs can be built on top of the lintel which means greater space can be enclosed and multiple levels added.

■ **postern**

the back door of a castle.

■ **postern gate**

a side or less important gate into a castle; usually for peacetime use by pedestrians.

■ **posticum**

also called Opisthodomos, a small room in the Cella of a Classical temple used as a treasury.

■ **postscaenuum**

Latin: the rooms behind the scaenae (stage house.)

■ **pot-life**

the time interval following the addition of an accelerator before chemically curing material will become too viscous to apply satisfactorily.

■ **pozzolana**

a rust coloured volcanic ash, found in the regions in central Italy around the town of Pozzuoli, which was a crucial component in Roman concrete.

■ **praecinctio**

Latin: something that surrounds or circles. The surrounding Roman corridor separating the galleries of a theatre; corresponds to the Greek 'diazomata'.

■ **praecinctiones**

roman passages for audience access to the cavea; according to Vitruvius, 'broad passages running between them and parallel to (the cavea) seating. These passages were called diazwvmata, or katatomaiv, Lat. praecinctiones....The number of passages (præcinctiones) must be regulated by the height of the theatre, and are not to be higher than their width, because if made higher, they will reflect and obstruct the voice in its passage upwards.'

■ **praetorium**

the residence of the Governor of a Roman province or Legion Commander.

■ **praxiteles**

Greek sculptor active from 370-330 BCE.

■ **prayer desk**

also called a prie-dieu, a prayer desk is a kneeler with a small shelf for books, as in the illustration on the right. In churches where it is customary to kneel for prayer, there might be two prayer desks in the chancel, one for the clergy and the other for the lay leader. Prayer desks are also found in private homes and small chapels.

precast

concrete building components which are formed and cured at a factory and then transported to a work site for erection.

predella

the narrow ledge on which an altarpiece rests on an altar.

predryer

a structure similar to a kiln that is sometimes used in the initial stages of drying.

predrying

a wood drying process carried out in a predryer before kiln drying.

presbytery

at the East end, East of the Choir but West of the retrochoir, home to the high altar.

preservative

any substance that is effective in preventing , for a reasonable period of time, the development and action of fungi, borer and insect attack in wood.

pre-shimed tape sealant

a sealant having a pre-formed shape containing solids or discrete particles that limit its deformation under compression.

pressed brick

prior to being placed in a kiln for hardening, the clay is pressed to create sharp edges and a smooth surface.

pressure

pressure is a similar idea to stress, the force intensity at a point, except that pressure means something acting on the surface of an object rather than within the material of the object. When discussing the pressure within a fluid, the meaning is equivalent to stress.

pressure-reducing valve

valve installed in the water service line where it enters the building to reduce the pressure of water in the line to an acceptable pressure used in buildings (40-55 psi desired).

pressure-relief valve

valve to relieve excess pressure in water storage tanks.

pressure-treated lumber

lumber that is treated in such a way that the sealer is forced into the pores of the wood.

presurfacing

surfacing of both broad faces of green rough sawn timber intended to permit drying by a schedule more severe than the prescribed schedule for rough sawn timber, achieving faster drying and fewer drying defects.

pretreatment - steaming

a process sometimes carried out before commencing a drying schedule. The timber is subjected to atmospheric pressure steam. It is often carried out to fix or enhance colour.

■ primer

a material of relatively thin consistency applied to a surface for the purpose of creating a more secure bonding surface and to form a barrier to prevent migration of components, the first coat of paint in a paint job that consists of two or more coats, the paint used for such a first coat.

■ priming

sealing of a porous surface so that compounds will not stain, lose elasticity, shrink excessively, etc. because of loss of oil or vehicle into the surround.

■ principia

in a Roman castrum or fortification where the Standard of the Legion were kept. It was also a place of meeting.

■ prohedria

(pl. prohedriai) seat of honour directly in front of or around the orchestra; in the Greek theatre, prohedriai were honorific seats reserved particularly for priests, notably the priest of Dionysus, and dignitaries.

■ projection

in roofing, any object or equipment which pierces the roof membrane.

■ pronaos

in a Classical temple, an open vestibule before the Cella. Also called Anticum.

■ propylaea

the ancient Greek structure that is both literally and symbolically the gate to the sacred precinct. At the Acropolis in Athens, the propylaea contained a library and a picture gallery providing a place to rest after the steep climb, an a place to prepare oneself for worship. It is from the propylaea that the view of the sacred precinct is planned. From this vantage point a 3/4 view of each important building is possible.

■ propylon

an enormous entrance built to protect the main artery in and out of an ancient city or sanctuary.

■ proskenion

Greek: (proscaenium) (proskênion) Also called the okribas; front wall of the stage (logeion); an acting area which projected in front of the skene (the word proskenion means 'something set up before the skene'); in Classical Greek theatre, the ground-level portion immediately in front of the skene was used as an acting area; in Hellenistic period, the proskenion was a raised platform in front of the skene; the skene eventually included two levels, a lower level with a roof (the Hellenistic logeion or stage) and the second story skene with openings for entrances (thyromata).

protection board

in roofing, heavy asphalt impregnated boards which are laid over bituminous coatings to protect against mechanical injury.

prow

acute-angled projection.

psarotaverna

a Taverna specialising in fish and seafood. Usually found on or near the beach.

psistaria

a Taverna specialising in meats grilled on a spit.

psychrometric charts

a psychrometric chart or psychrometric table relates dry bulb temperature, wet bulb depression and humidity.

puddled

made waterproof.

pulpit

in churches with a historic floor plan, there are two speaker's stands in the front of the church. The one on the left (as viewed by the congregation) is called the pulpit. It is used by clergy to read the gospel and preach the sermon. Since the gospel lesson is usually read from the pulpit, the pulpit side of the church is called the gospel side. See **ambo and lectern.** In some churches, the positions of the pulpit and the lectern are reversed (that is, pulpit is on the right and the lectern is on the left) for architectural or aesthetic reasons.

pulpitum

Latin: a stage. Roman stage (logeion in the Greek theatre); a platform for a public speaker in front of the scaenae (scaenae frons); Vitruvius gives the maximum height as five feet as opposed to the ten to twelve feet of the Hellenistic logeion.

purlin

one of a series of horizontal framing timbers supporting the rafters or spanning between trusses or frames and supporting the roof. Purlins usually span at right angles to the slope of the roof.

purlins

a roof construction in which [pieces of timber] are laid between the principal rafters; they support the boards that run between the ridge and eaves of the roof. Purlins help support the roofing material. In Craftsman architecture, the purlins frequently project from the wall into the eaves.

push - pull racking

a method for building racks where alternative boards in alternative layers are kept flush with alternate ends. This gives a checkerboard arrangement at the ends of the rack. It is also called topping & tailing.

■ **push stick**

in hardware, a tool used when cutting a short board on a table saw.

■ **putlog**

beams placed in holes to support a hoarding; horizontal scaffold beam.

■ **putlog hole**

a hole intentionally left in the surface of a wall for insertion of a horizontal pole.

■ **putty**

a type of cement usually made of whiting and boiled linseed oil, beaten or kneaded to the consistency of dough, and used in sealing glass in sash, filling small holes and crevices in wood, and for similar purposes.

■ **pyramid**

In ancient Egypt, a quadrilateral masonry mass with steeply sloping sides meeting at an apex, used as a tomb.

■ **pyx**

a small box with a lid to contain the consecrated host. Compare with ciborium See **paten, chalice, monstrance.**

■ **quadrangle**

inner courtyard.

■ **quadrant vault**

is a half-barrel (tunnel) vault.

■ **quadriga**

a four horse chariot.

■ **quadripartite rib vault**

a rib vault which is divided into four sections by two diagonal ribs. See **rib vault.** Other types of rib vaults fan, net, sexpartite.

■ **quadripartite vault**

a vault in four equal-sized sections, comprising transverse, diagonal and wall ribs.

■ **quarry cut stone**

same as rough cut stone. Quarry cut stone has a rough finish unlike milled stone, which has a smooth finish.

■ **quarry sap**

the moisture found in most newly quarried stone which quickly dries out forming the case hardening.

■ **quarter cut**

a method of slicing veneers whereby the average inclination of the growth rings to the wide face is greater than 45 degrees.

■ **quarter round**

a small molding that has the cross section of a quarter circle.

■ **quarter sawn timber**

timber in which the average inclination of the growth rings to the wide face is not less than 45 degrees.

■ **quartersawn grain**

another term for edge grain.

■ **quatrefoil**

an ornamental form which has four lobes or foils. It may resemble a four-petaled flower.

■ **Queen Anne**

a style of architecture found in late 19th century America and

England. The floor plans are asymmetrical and the structures usually feature turrets, forward facing gables, cross gabled roofs, decorative wood and spindle designs and other highly ornate architectural elements.

quire

alternative spelling of Choir.

quirk

v-shaped nick.

quoin

pronounced 'coin.' In masonry construction, the brick or stone used to reinforce the corner of a wall. Sometimes a different or contrasting brick or stone is used for decoration. Also spelled coign or coin.

quoins

reinforcement at wall edges of a building, often in contrasting masonry (size and colour) from the rest of the building.

rabbet

a rectangular longitudinal groove cut in the corner edge of a board or plank.

rack

a unit of timber where each layer is separated and spaced for drying with rack sticks.

rack stick

a strip of wood or another material that is placed between rows of timber or other wood products in a rack. Rack sticks are placed at right angles to the long axis of the timber to permit air to circulate between the layers. Also referred to as 'sticker' or 'stripper'.

racking

the distortion of a rectangular shape to a skewed parallelogram.

racking frame

a combination of guides and supports that help produce good stick alignment and square sides and ends in hand built racks.

radial

coincident with a radius from the axis of the tree or log to the circumference.

radial saw

a circular saw which hangs from a horizontal arm or beam and slides back and forth. The arm pivots from side to side to allow for angle cuts and bevels. When sawing finish plywood, the good side should face up as the saw cuts on the down stroke.

radially sawn

timber sawn on the radius from the central axis of the tree or log to the circumference, perpendicular to the growth rings. The resulting pieces are generally triangular in shape.

radiant heating

a method of heating, usually consisting of a forced hot water system with pipes placed in the floor, wall, or ceiling; or with electrically heated panels.

radiation

any heated surface loses heat to cooler surrounding space or surfaces through radiation. The earth receives its heat from the sun by radiation. The heat rays are turned into heat as they strike an object which will absorb some or all of the heat transmitted.

■ **radiator**

a heating unit which is supplied heat through a hot water system.

■ **rafter**

1. one of a series of roof support timbers that provide principal support for the roofing material. Rafters usually span parallel to the slope of the roof.
2. a sloping roof member that supports the roof covering which extends from the ridge or the hip of the roof to the eaves. A common rafter is one which runs square with the plate and extends to the ridge. A hip rafter extends from the outside angle of the plate towards the apex of the roof. They are 2' deeper or wider than common rafters. A valley rafter extends from an inside angle of the plates toward the ridge of the house.

■ **rafter tails**

projection of roof rafters beyond the wall, under the eaves of a building.

■ **rafters**

any of the beams that slope from the ridge of a roof to the eaves and serve to support the roof.

■ **raggle block**

a specially designed masonry block having a slot or opening into which the top edge of the roof flashing is inserted and anchored.

■ **rail**

cross members of panel doors or of a sash. Also the upper and lower members of a balustrade or staircase extending from one vertical support, such as a post, to another.

■ **rake**

trim members that run parallel to the roof slope and form the finish between the wall and a gable roof extension. The angle of slope of a roof rafter, or the inclined portion of a cornice.

■ **rampart**

defensive stone or earth wall surrounding castle.

■ **rankin**

thermometer scale on which unit of measurement equals the Fahrenheit degree.

■ **rath**

low, circular ring work.

■ **ravelin**

outwork with two faces forming a salient angle; like in a star-shaped fort.

■ **raw linseed oil**

the crude product processed from flaxseed and usually without much subsequent treatment.

■ **ray**

a fissure radiating from the centre of the heartwood outwards, In which protein is stored.

■ **rays**

a ribbon-like arrangement of cells, usually oriented in the radial direction.

reaction

a reaction is a force exerted by a support on an object sometimes called support reaction. Using this definition, a reaction is an external force.

rear-arch

arch on the inner side of a wall.

rebar

reinforcing bar used to increase the tensile strength of concrete.

rebetika

rebetika music is a type of music that is distinctly Greek yet no one knows quite where it came from. Its earliest forms could not have been sung before about 1850, but it was the refugees from Asia Minor in the 1920's who popularised it. To this day, you will see young and old people alike singing or mouthing the words to these songs when they are played in restaurants, clubs, and cafes. The word also refers to restaurants that serve traditional Greek food and have live rebetika bands.

reconditioner

a chamber into which wet steam (not more than 100°C) is injected for several hours to recondition timber.

reconditioning treatment

a high temperature/high relative humidity (100%) treatment applied after drying to restore the shape of collapsed or distorted wood.

recorder - controller

an instrument that continuously records dry- and wet-bulb temperatures of circulated air in a dryer or kiln and regulates these conditions by activating automatic heat and humidification systems.

rectilinear

characterised by straight lines as opposed to curvilinear which is characterised by curved lines.

red-figure technique

an ancient method of decorating ceramic vessels. Developed by the Greeks about 525 BCE., the process results in red figures on a shiny black background.

redoubt

small self-contained fieldwork, a refuge for soldiers outside the main defences.

redry

in kiln or veneer drying, a process whereby dried material found to have a moisture content level higher than desired is returned to the dryer for additional drying.

reeded

parallel convex mouldings.

re-entrant

recessed; opposite of salient.

refectory

a dining room in a monastery. other parts of monastery chapter house, cloister, scriptorium.

reflective glass

glass with a metallic coating to reduce solar heat gain.

reflective insulation

sheet material with one or both sun faces of comparatively low heat emissivity, such as aluminium foil. When used in building construction the surfaces face air spaces, reducing the radiation across the air space.

register

a fixture through which conditioned air flows. In a gravity heating system, it is located near the baseboard. In an air conditioning system, it is located close to the thermostat.

reglet

a horizontal slot, formed or cut in a parapet or other masonry wall, into which the top edge of counterflashing can be inserted and anchored. In glazing, a reglet is typically a pocket or keyway extruded into the framing for installing the glazing gaskets.

rehabilitation

returning a building to a useful state, but not necessarily returning it to an original, or restored state.

reinforced concrete

a combination of steel and concrete using the best properties of each. The steel consists of rebar or reinforcing bars varying from 3/8 ' to 2 1/4 'in diameter and is placed before concrete is poured.

reinforced masonry

masonry units, reinforcing steel, grout and/or mortar combined to act together to strengthen the masonry structure.

reinforcing

1. steel rods or metal fabric placed in concrete slabs, beams, or columns to increase their strength.
file structure
2. a computerised file in which the fields that combine to make up a record are held in a number of files, or tables. This type of structure is well suited to applications that require the ability to relate and combine pieces of information held in a number of files for purposes of both searching and retrieval. In a relational structure any hierarchical relationships between elements of records can be modelled explicitly and reproduced in the structure. (In flat files these relationships are implicit.) A relational data structure also allows for multiple occurrences of individual fields or groups of fields.

relative heat gain

the amount of heat gain through a glass product taking into consideration the effects of solar heat gain (shading coefficient) and conductive heat gain (U-value.)

relative humidity

at a given temperature, this is the amount of moisture in air as a percentage of the maximum moisture carrying capacity of the air, i.e. the water vapour pressure as a percentage of the saturated water vapour pressure.

relief

moldings and ornamentation projecting from the surface of a wall.

relieving arch

1. an arch which encloses an arch or a window or other opening. It helps relieve some of the weight on the arch of the opening. Compare with blind arch.
2. a supportive arch constructed within a wall to absorb weight upon a passageway or portal below.

reliquary

a container for relics. Often reliquaries were in the form of caskets, though it was quite common for them to be shaped like statues or body parts (such as hands or heads.) Compare with monstrance.

renaissance

styles existing in Italy in the fifteenth and sixteenth centuries; adaptations of ancient Roman elements to contemporary uses, with attention to the principles of Vitruvius and to existing ruins. Symmetry, simplicity, and exact mathematical relationships are emphasised.

reredos

1. a decorative screen situated to the rear of the altar.
2. carved screen behind the Altar, often depicting Christ and the Disciples.

resins

a class of amorphous vegetable substances secreted by certain plants or trees.

resistance

the internal structure of wires even in the best conductors opposes the flow of electric current and converts some current into heat. This internal friction-like effect is called resistance and is measured in ohms. Resistance equals voltage divided by amperage.

resorcinol glue

a glue that is high in both wet and dry strength and resistant to high temperatures. It is used for gluing lumber or assembly joints that must withstand severe service conditions.

respond

half-pier bonded into a wall to carry an arch.

restoration

when a building is brought back to its original, or near original state.

resultant

the resultant of a system of forces is a single force or moment whose magnitude, direction, and location make it statically equivalent to the system of forces.

retable

1. an altarpiece, decorated with painting or sculpture which stands at the back of an altar.
2. an architectural screen or wall above and behind an altar, usually containing painting, sculpture, carving or other decorations.

reticulated tracery

a tessellated tracery pattern comprising circles with ogee-shaped points top and bottom.

retirata

1. improvised fieldwork to counter an imminent breach.
2. the recovery of information from storage. The retrievability of information is determined to a large extent by the care which has been taken to make it retrievable through such means as terminology control and the design of data structure.

retrochoir

the area of the church to the east of the presbytery.

retsina

a cheap Greek wine made with tree resin.

return

In heating and cooling systems, a vent that returns cold air to be warmed. In a hot air furnace system, it is located near an inside wall.

reveal

the surface left exposed when one board is fastened over another; the edge of the upper set slightly back from the edge of the lower.

reverberation

the persistent echoing of sound within an enclosure after the original source of the sound has stopped, due to repeated reflection between the enclosing surfaces.

revetment

retaining wall to prevent erosion; to face a surface with stone slabs.

rhyolite

a type of granite found in Colorado and used broadly around the State as a building material. It is perhaps one of the most common local masonry material used.

rib

1. an arch of masonry, often molded, which forms part of the framework on which a vault rests. Ribs generally project from the undersurface of the vault. See also rib vault Types of ribs diagonal rib, lierne, ridge rib, tierceron, transverse rib Compare with infilling or webbing.
2. a relatively slender, molded masonry arch that projects from a surface. In Gothic architecture, the ribs form the framework of the vaulting.

rib vault

a masonry vault with a relatively thin web and set within a framework of ribs. Types of rib vaults fan, net, quadripartite, sexpartite Compare with barrel or tunnel vault, groin vault.

ribbed vault

there is a framework of ribs or arches under the intersections of the vaulting sections.

ribbon (or girt)

normally a 1 by 4-inch board let into the studs horizontally to support ceiling or second-floor joists.

ribbon figure

a striped figure produced by cutting timber that has an interlocked grain. Also called striped figure.

ridge
1. the highest part of the roof at the meeting of the upper ends of the common rafters.
2. the horizontal line at the junction of the top edges of two sloping roof surfaces.

ridge beam
a beam located at the highest part of the roof to support the upper ends of the common rafters.

ridge board
the board placed on edge at the ridge of the roof into which the upper ends of the rafters are fastened.

ridge rib
the rib running along the apex of a vault.

ridge rib or longitudinal ridge rib
a rib which runs down the apex of the vault in a longitudinal direction. other types of ribs: diagonal, lierne, tierceron, transverse rib. See **rib vault.**

rigid
an idealised concept meaning something which does not deform under loading. In fact, all objects deform under loading, but in modelling it can be useful to idealise very stiff objects as rigid.

rigid connection
see **fixed connection.**

rigid metal conduit
this conduit resembles plumbing pipe, protecting wires from damage.

ringwork
circular earthwork of bank and ditch.

rip
to cut along the grain.

rise
vertical height between springing line and underside of keystone.

rise (of an arch or a vault)
the vertical distance between the spring line of an arch or vault and the keystone or boss. See **boss, keystone, span, spring line.**

riser
each of the vertical boards closing the spaces between the treads of stairways.

rococo
a style originating in France c. 1720, developed out of Baroque types, and characterised by its ornamentation of shell work, foliage, etc., and its refined use of different materials, such as stucco, metal, or wood for a delicate effect.

roll
moulding of semi-circular section.

roll roofing
roofing material, composed of fibre and satin rated with asphalt, that is supplied in 36-inch wide rolls with 108 square feet of material. Weights are generally 45 to 90 pounds per roll.

roller support
in two dimensions, a roller support restrains one translation degree of freedom.

Roman period

the Romans ruled Greece from 146 BCE. - 324 A.D. when they sacked Corinth and defeated the Achaean League, a remnant of Alexander the Great's conquered territories. Mark Anthony was the first ruler and Greece flourished under Rome's influence.

Romanesque

1. a style developed in western and southern Europe after 1000 characterised by heavy masonry and the use of the round arch, barrel and groin vaults, narrow openings, and the vaulting rib, the vaulting shaft, and central and western towers.
2. the prevailing architectural style, 8-12th cent.; massive masonry, round arches, small windows, groin-and barrel-vault.
3. a style of European architecture containing both Roman and Byzantine elements, prevalent especially in the 11th and 12th centuries and characterised by thick walls, barrel vaults, and relatively unrefined ornamentation.

Romanesque revival/ richarsonian Romanesque

a style popular in the late 19th century (1890s) featuring massive proportions, curved arches often in clusters, use of rough cut masonry, slate or tile roofs, and parapeted gable ends and other elements that would add to its grand style. It is a style that was first promoted by Henry Hobson Richardson (1838-1886) and carried on by his many followers. Typically, the style is primarily used for public buildings, churches, university buildings and railroad terminals.

romex

a non-metallic sheathed cable consisting of two or more insulated conductors having an outer sheath of moisture resistant, non-metallic material. The conductor insulation is rubber, neoprene, thermoplastic or a moisture resistant flame retardant fibrous material. There are two types: NM and NMC

rood

a large crucifix (Christ on the cross) usually over the entrance to the chancel. A rood tower or spire is one situated over the crossing.

rood screen

screen between choir and nave, often elaborate. Carries a cross, as rood comes from the Latin for cross.

roof batten

small timbers fixed to the top of rafters to which the roofing material is secured.

roof sheathing

the boards or sheet material fastened to the roof rafters on which the shingle or other roof covering is laid.

roof system

general term referring to the waterproof covering, roof insulation, vapour barrier, if used and roof deck as an entity.

roofridge

summit line of roof.

ropey figure

markings in the form of a twisted rope.

rose window

1. a circular window composed of patterned tracery arranged in petal-like formation.
2. the large, circular window with tracery and stained glass frequently used in the facades of Gothic churches.

rot

synonymous with decay, the softening, weakening, or total decomposition of wood substance by fungi. Brown - In wood, any decay caused by fungi that attack cellulose rather than lignin, producing a light to dark brown friable residue. Dry - A term loosely applied to any dry, crumbly rot but especially to rot that, when in an advanced stage, permits the wood to be crushed easily to a dry powder. The term is actually a misnomer for any decay, since all fungi require considerable moisture for growth. White - In wood, any decay caused by fungi that attack both cellulose and lignin, producing a generally whitish residue that may be spongy or stringy or occur in pockets.

rotary-cut veneer

veneer cut in a lathe which rotates a log chucked in the centre against a knife. This method of peeling is used to produce decorative veneers and is a common method of manufacturing veneers for plywood.

rotation

motion of an object where the path of every point is a circle or circular arc. A rotation is defined by a point and vector which determine the axis of rotation. The direction of the vector is the direction of the axis and the magnitude of the vector is the angle of rotation.

rotunda

domed building, circular in plan, such as the Pantheon.

rough

in hardware, metal fastenings on cabinets which are usually concealed, like staples.

rough opening

the opening in a wall into which a door or window is to be installed.

rough plumbing

all plumbing that should be done before the finish trades (sheetrock, painting, etc), including all waste lines and supply water lines that are in the walls or framing of the building. See **plumbing, sub rough, and finish plumbing.**

rough sawn

surface condition of wood as it leaves the saw, i.e. not dressed or final sawn.

round timber

timber used in the original round form, such as in poles, posts or bridge beams.

rout

to cut out by gouging.

RPM

Revolutions Per Minute.

rubber emulsion paint

paint, the vehicle of which consists of rubber or synthetic rubber dispersed in fine droplets in water.

rubber-tired roller

a roller with rubber tires commonly used for compacting trimmed subgrade or aggregate base or clay type soils.

rubble

fill; unsquared stone not laid in courses.

run

the horizontal distance between the eaves and the ridge of the roof, being half the span for a symmetrical gable roof. (stairs) The net width of a step or the horizontal distance covered by a flight of stairs.

rusticated or rustication

stone masonry construction in which the faces of the blocks are rough and the individual blocks are separated by deep joints. Depending on the texture of the rock surface, rusticated blocks may be sorted as smooth, cyclopean (rock-faced), diamond-pointed, or vermiculated.

rustication

1. worked ashlar stone with the faces left rough.
2. heavy stonework with a surface left rough, or with deeply channelled joints, used principally on Renaissance buildings.

r-value

the thermal resistance of a glazing system. The R-value is the reciprocal of the U-value. The higher the R value, the less heat is transmitted throughout the glazing material.

saber saw

a saw that cuts on the upstroke, good side of wood faces down.

sacred precinct

in ancient Greek cities, the area reserved solely for religious worship, usually located on the highest ground, and surrounded by a wall. Entry was through the propylaea. The precinct contained temples, shrines, statues and treasuries. The plan or layout of all of the structures is based on a system of polar coordinates.

sacristy

in historic church architecture, the sacristy is the room or closet in which communion equipment, linen, and supplies are kept. It is usually equipped with a sink.

saddle

two sloping surfaces meeting in a horizontal ridge, used between the back side of a chimney, or other vertical surface, and a sloping roof.

salient

wall projection, arrowhead.

sally-port

small heavily fortified side door from which the defenders can rush out, strike, and retire.

saltire

diagonal, equal-limbed cross.

sample board

a representative piece of timber of a known moisture content that is placed in a stack, or a predryer or kiln charge, so that it may be removed for comparative examination, weighing, or testing during the drying process.

sanctuary

in historic church architecture, the front part of the church from which the service is conducted, as distinct from the nave, where the congregation sits. The sanctuary is usually an elevated platform, usually three steps up from the nave. In churches with a lecture-hall floor plan, the term 'sanctuary' is often used to mean both chancel and nave because the two are not architecturally distinct. In historic usage, chancel; and sanctuary are synonyms.

sand float finish

lime mixed with sand, resulting in a textured finish.

sap

the fluid in green wood that contains nutrients and other chemicals in solution.

sapwood

1. outer layers of wood which, in a growing tree, contain living cells and reserve materials such as starch. Under most conditions the sapwood is paler in colour and more susceptible to decay than heartwood.
2. beneath the bark. The centre is a darker colour and is known as heartwood. Water and minerals travel up the tree through the sapwood which contains living cells. Heartwood has no living cells. Because sapwood is more permeable, it is more susceptible to decay. Shrinkage does occur in timber, but nearly always in section, very rarely along a length. Most good quality woods are better (and easier) worked green, but where precision is required in for example, door construction, the wood should be well seasoned. Most of the problems of swelling, shrinkage and decay associated with timber stem from moisture content, which can vary between 12-25% over a season depending on where and how it is used. Wood is mainly composed of cellulose (65%) which gives strength, and lignin (35%) which gives hardness. The common analogy is that of a frozen sponge where cellulose represented the fibres, lignin the ice. Timber is sold by the cubic metre, the price varying depending on quality and species. A metre cube

however is a lot of wood, and when considering the amount of timber in say, a sash and case window, price should not be an argument for accepting poor quality. Timber can be pre-treated against rot and insect attack. The most common treatment is CCA, Copper Chrome/Arsenic which sounds alarming, but is generally held to be safe, because the chemicals used do not leech out, various brand names exist for this process, cellcured, tanalised etc.

■ sarcophagus

a stone coffin, often bearing sculpture, inscriptions, etc. Compare with mausoleum, memorial brass.

■ sash

a single light frame containing one or more lights of glass.

■ sash balance

a device, usually operated by a spring or tensioned weather stripping designed to counterbalance double-hung window sash.

■ saturated felt

a felt which is impregnated with tar or asphalt.

■ satyr

a half man, half animal follower of Dionysus.

■ sawed veneer

veneer produced by sawing.

■ sawing

logs can be sawn into boards or planks in two basic ways, either by cutting straight through from one side to the other, known as plain or flat sawn, or to cut in a radial direction where the rings meet the board at an angle of more than 45 degrees. Plain sawn timber is more prone to cupping and is less durable when used as flooring. The circular saw was invented in 1777. Pit saws where the log was positioned over a pit with a man above (lifting) and one below (guiding) was the traditional method of sawing timber along its length. The man below got filthy, and while the man above worked harder he was 'top dog' the origin of the expression. While on the subject of sayings, timber was first sawn on trestles, the log was balanced at its centre, one end was raised and sawn, and then the process was repeated to the other end.

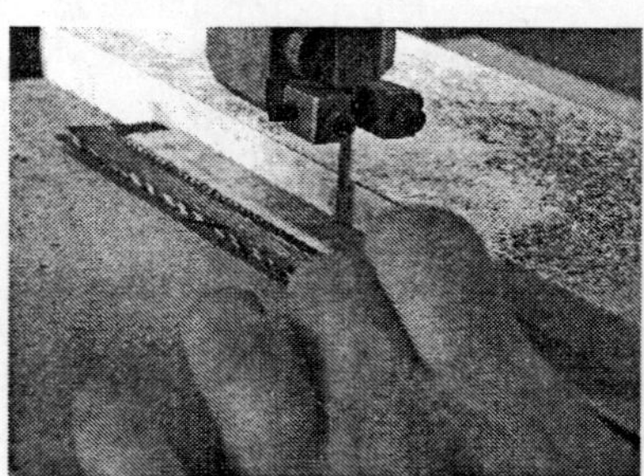

■ sawn timber

timber finished to size with a saw.

■ scaenae

Latin: theatre stage or scene, in the Roman theatre usually referring to the stage house or building behind the stage; corresponds to the Hellenistic skene.

■ scaenae frons

Latin: front of the façade of the stage house or 'scaenae', pierced by three to five doors; unadorned in earlier theatres, but became increasingly ornate by the 2nd century with the addition of columns, niches, and statues decorating up to three stories of architecture.

■ **scaffolding**

the temporary wooden frame work built next to a wall to support both workers and materials.

■ **scalar**

a mathematical entity which has a numeric value but no direction (in contrast to a vector.)

■ **scale**

carving resembling overlapping fish scales.

■ **scale, drawing scale, drawing to scale**

an exact drawn representation of a building is possible through the use of a scale (mathematical or graphic) showing the relationship of the smaller measurement to the larger. For example a plan drawing may be drawn to a scale of 1' (inch) on the drawing, equals 8' (feet) in the actual building.

■ **scallop**

carved in a series of semi-circles.

■ **scappled**

cut to a smooth face.

■ **scarf joint**

a joint made by bonding two matching bevelled ends or edges.

■ **scarp**

slope on inner side of ditch.

■ **scratch coat**

the first coat of plaster, which is scratched to form a bond for the second coat.

■ **screed or screeding**

the wood or metal straightedge used to strike off or level newly placed concrete when doing cement work. Screeds can be the levelling device used or the form work used to level or establish the level of the concrete. Screeds can be hand used or mechanical.

■ **screen facade**

a facade which is so highly decorated with sculpture or other decorative elements that it acts as a screen placed in front of the facade. It may seem to hide the face of the building from view. Compare with narthex, westwork. See **west end.**

■ **scribe**

to mark for an irregular cut.

■ **scribing**

fitting woodwork to an irregular surface. In moldings, cutting the end of one piece to fit the molded face of the other at an interior angle to replace a miter joint.

scriptorium

area in a monastery where books and documents were written, copied, and illuminated. Other parts of monastery chapter house, cloister, refectory segmented dome or cloister vault. A dome placed over a polygonal base. It is not a semi-sphere, but is formed of curved sections which correspond to the parts of the polygon on which it rests. Compare with squinch.

scriptorium

a Medieval writing room in which scrolls were also housed.

scupper

an outlet in the wall of a building or a parapet wall for drainage of water from a flat roof.

scutch

a bricklayer's cutting tool used for dressing and trimming brick to a special shape. It resembles a small pick.

sealant

an elastomeric material with adhesive qualities applied between components of a similar or dissimilar nature to provide an effective barrier against the passage of the elements.

sealed-combustion appliances

appliances with the ignition heating element sealed and vented to prevent gases from mixing with and polluting indoor air quality.

sealer

a finishing material, either clear or pigmented, that is usually applied directly over uncoated wood for the purpose of sealing the surface.

seasoned timber

timber that has been dried so that the maximum moisture content anywhere in the piece does not exceed 15%.

seasoning

drying timber to a moisture content appropriate to the conditions and purposes for which it is to be used.

seasoning stresses

stresses in timber caused by variation in shrinkage as it dries.

secondary façade

a facade with an entrance, not facing the street or primary roadway.

section

in architecture, a drawing showing a vertical slice through a building. A longitudinal section is a cut down the length of the building, a cross section cuts across the shorter dimension of the building . All horizontal and vertical lines are drawn to a scale. In detailed section drawings the interior is shown in elevation.

section modulus

a property of a cross sectional shape, which depends on shape, and orientation. Section modulus is usually denoted S, and S = I/c, where I = moment of inertia about an axis through the centroid, and c is the distance from the centroid to the extreme edge of the section.

segmental

less than a semi-circle.

self-healing

a term used to describe to a material which melts with the heat from the sun's rays, and seals over cracks that were earlier formed from other causes. Some waterproof membranes are self-healing.

self-levelling

a term used to describe a viscous material that is applied by pouring. In its uncured state, it spreads out evenly.

selvage

the unsurfaced strip along a sheet of roll roofing which forms the under portion at the lap in the application of the roof covering.

semi-arch

an arch where only one part of its span is complete as for example in a flying buttress.

semi-dome

a half dome. Compare with dome.

semigloss (paint or enamel)

a paint or enamel made with a slight insufficiency of non-volatile vehicle so that its coating, when dry, has some lustre but is not very glossy.

separation

in concrete application, what happens to concrete when it is dropped directly with a flat chute causing the concrete to separate, usually occurring at a 1:2 slope.

service conductor

in electrical contracting, the supply conductors that extend from the street main or from the transformer to the service equipment.

service drop

in electrical contracting, the overhead service conductors from the last pole or other aerial support to and including the splices, if any, connecting to the service entrance conductors at the building.

set

permanent deformation in wood that occurs during drying when the tensile and compressive stress exceeds its elastic limit. Set prevents normal shrinkage of the timber and can lead to more obvious defects such as casehardening. Compression - Set that occurs during compression, which tends to give the wood a smaller than normal dimension after drying. Compression set is usually found in the inner layers of wood during the later stages of drying, but sometimes occurs in the outer layers after extended conditioning or rewetting. Tension - Set that occurs during tension, which tends to increase the dimensions of the wood after drying. Tension set usually occurs in the outer layers of wood during drying.

■ **set back/off**

ledge on wall face.

■ **setting blocks**

generally rectangular cured extrusions of neoprene, EPDM, silicone, rubber or other suitable material on which the glass product bottom edge is placed to effectively support the weight of the glass.

■ **sexpartile vault**

is a rib vault with six panels.

■ **sexpartite rib vault**

1. a rib vault which is divided into six sections.
2. a rib vault whose surface is divided into six sections by three ribs. See **rib vault Other types of rib vaults fan, net, quadripartite.**

■ **sexpartite vault**

a six-section vault, typically a quadripartite vault with an additional transverse rib.

■ **shading coefficient**

the ratio of the solar heat gain through a specific glass product to the solar heat gain through a lite of 1/8' (3mm) clear glass. Glass of 1/8' (3mm) thickness is given a value of 1.0, therefore the shading coefficient of a glass product is calculated as follows:

■ **shaft**

the structural member which serves as the main support of a column or pier. The shaft is between the capital and the base. See abacus or impost block, base, capital, column, pier.

■ **shake**

separation or breakage of the wood fibres caused by stresses in the standing tree or by felling and handling of the log. It is not caused by shrinkage during drying.

■ **shakes**

splits along a ray in a piece of timber. They do not usually affect the strength of the material but can cause distortion, particularly if the timber suddenly becomes wet. Cup shakes are splits separating the annual rings.

■ **shear**

an system of internal forces whose resultant is a force acting perpendicular to the longitudinal axis of a structural member or assembly sometimes called shear force.

■ **shear**

a condition of stress or strain where parallel planes slide relative to each other.

■ **shear connector**

usually metal connectors fitted inside a timber joint to transfer shear across a wide area of grain.

■ **shear modulus**

the ratio of shear stress divided by the corresponding shear strain in a linear elastic material.

shear panel

a selection of wall designed to resist lateral forces acting in, or parallel to, the plane of the wall.

shear strain

strain measuring the intensity of racking in the material. Shear strain is measured as the change in angle of the corners of a small square of material.

shear stress

stress acting parallel to an imaginary plane cut through an object.

sheathing

the structural covering, usually wood boards, plywood, gypsum or wood fibre, used over studs or rafters of framed buildings as the first layer of outer wall covering nailed to the studs or rafters.

sheathing paper

a building material, generally paper or felt, used in wall and roof construction as a protection against the passage of air and sometimes moisture.

shed addition

shed refers to the type of roof, which has a single sloping surface. A shed addition would be an added structure to an existing building with this type of roof as a primary element.

shed dormer

a dormer window whose eave line is parallel to the eave line of the main roof instead of being gabled.

shed roof

a roof having only one slope or pitch, with only one set of rafters which fall from a higher to a lower wall.

sheet metal connector

a shaped connector made of sheet metal and perforated so that nails can be driven through.

sheet metal work

all components of a house employing sheet metal, such as flashing, gutters, and downspouts.

sheetrock

panels made primarily from gypsum installed over the framing to form the interior walls and ceilings. Sheetrock is often called gypsum board.

shelf-life

used in the glazing and sealant business to refer to the length of time a product may be stored before beginning to lose its effectiveness. Manufacturers usually state the shelf life and the necessary storage conditions on the package.

shell keep

circular or oval wall surrounding inner portion of castle.

■ **shellac**

a transparent coating made by dissolving lac, a resinous secretion of the lac bug (a scale insect that thrives in tropical countries, especially India), in alcohol.

■ **shell-keep**

circular or oval wall surrounding inner portion of castle; usually stores and accommodations inside the hollow walls.

■ **shell-keep**

the circular or oval wall surrounding inner portion of castle.

■ **shingle siding**

roofing type shingles used as siding, often cut to form patterns such as fish scales, or diamonds.

■ **shingles**

roof covering of asphalt, wood, tile, slate, or other material cut to stock lengths, widths, and thicknesses, which are laid in a series of overlapping rows as a roof covering on pitched roofs.

■ **shiplap lumber**

lumber that is edge-dressed to make a close rebated or lapped joint.

■ **shore 'a' hardness**

measure of firmness of a compound by means of a Durometer Hardness Gauge. (A hardness range of 20-25 is about the firmness of an art gum eraser. A hardness of about 90 is about the firmness of a rubber heel.)

■ **shoring**

a temporary support erected in a trench or other excavation to support the walls from caving in.

■ **shrinkage**

the reduction in dimension or volume which takes place in timber when the moisture content is reduced below fibre saturation point, expressed as a percentage of the original dimensions or volume. Linear shrinkage occurs in three directions radial, tangential and longitudinal.

■ **shutter**

usually lightweight louvered or flush wood or nonwood frames in the form of doors located at each side of a window. Some are made to close over the window for protection; others are fastened to the wall as a decorative device.

■ **sidelights**

narrow windows installed vertically around a door.

■ **siding**

the finish covering of the outside wall of a frame building, whether made of horizontal weatherboards, vertical boards with battens, shingles, or other material.

siege

surrounding and attacking a castle, usually, a prolonged attack.

sight line

the line along the perimeter of glazing infills corresponding to the top edge of stationary and removable stops. The line to which sealants contacting the glazing infill are sometimes finished off.

silicone sealant

a sealant having as its chemical compound a backbone consisting of alternating silicon-oxygen atoms.

sill

1. lower horizontal face of an opening.
2. the horizontal support below a window or a door.
3. the bottom member of a door or window frame. It is usually angled to shed water.
4. the lowest member of the frame of a structure, resting on the foundation and supporting the floor joists or the uprights of the wall. The member forming the lower side of an opening, as a door sill, window sill. etc.

sill course

a strip of masonry that is set at the sill level of a building and usually has a greater projection than the surrounding masonry. If the masonry of a building is painted, the sill course will often be painted a contrasting colour as an accent. Sometimes called a stringcourse.

sill plate

1. the structural member forming the bottom of a rough opening for a door or window.
2. the framing member anchored to the foundation wall upon which studs and other framing members will be attached. It is the bottom plate of your exterior walls.

sill sealer

a material placed between the top of the foundation wall and the sill plate. Usually a foam strip, the sill sealer helps make a better fit and eliminate water problems.

sill step

the first step coming directly off a building at the door openings.

sima

this was usually only on the sides of the temple and had two main functions: it was there to hold the rainwater and it served as a decorative crowning to the building. In many temples it was also there to catch the run-off from the roof. For this purpose, it had equally spaced pipes or lion-head water spouts. On temples of the 4th century BCE., the sima had relief decorations of plants.

■ **Single Family Dwelling (SFD)**

a house built for the purpose of a single family as opposed to multi families such as a duplex or apartment complex.

■ **single ply**

a descriptive term signifying a roof membrane composed of only one layer of material such as EPDM, Hypalon or PVC.

■ **single tee**

the name given to a type of precast concrete deck which has one stiffening rib integrally cast into slab.

■ **skene**

Greek or Hellenistic building behind the orchestra (skene translates to 'tent' or 'hut'), originally used for storage but provided a convenient backing for performances; corresponds to the Roman scaenae a volume of drawings, watercolours, or works in other media applied directly to bound supports or pages.

■ **skillion roof**

a monoslope (single pitched) roof without a ridge or peak, providing the main roof or part of a roof

■ **sky dome**

a type of skylight exhibiting a characteristic translucent plastic domed top.

■ **skylight**

a structure on a roof that is designed to admit light and is somewhat above the plane of the roof surface.

■ **slab on grade**

a type of construction in which footings are needed but little or no foundation wall is poured.

■ **slag**

a by-product of smelting ore such as iron, lead or copper. Also overburden/dropping from welding which may burn, melt, or discolour adjacent surfaces.

■ **slate**

a dark grey stratified stone cut relatively thin and installed on pitched roofs in a shingle like fashion.

■ **sleeper**

1. lowest horizontal timber (or low wall).
2. usually, a wood member embedded in concrete, as in a floor, that serves to support and to fasten sub floor or flooring.

■ sliced veneer

veneer that is sliced off a log or flitch with a knife.

■ sling

a unit of timber. Synonymous with pack.

■ slits

narrow opening in a wall through which defenders can fire arrows at attackers.

■ slope

incline or pitch of roof surface.

■ sloped glazing

any installation of glass that is at a slope of 15 degrees or more from vertical.

■ slump-test

measures the consistency of a concrete mix or its stiffness. If the tests results are high, one likely cause would be too much water. Low slump-not enough water. The test is measured in inches.

■ socle

1. stone support for columns.
2. a low projecting base for a wall or statue. See **jamb figures, trumeau figure.**

■ soffit

1. underside of arch, hung parapet, or opening.
2. the underside of an arch, opening, or projecting architectural element See also arch. Other parts of an arch keystone, springer, voussoir.
3. the underside of an arch, beam, cornice, lintel, vault, or other overhead construction.

■ softening point

the temperature at which a substance changes from a hard material to a softer and more viscous material.

■ softwood

a general term for timber of trees classified botanically as Gymnosperm. Commercial timbers of this group are nearly all conifers. The term has no reference to the relative hardness of the wood.

■ soil cover (or ground cover)

a light covering of plastic film, roll roofing, or similar material used over the soil in crawl spaces of buildings to minimise moisture permeation of the area.

■ soil stack

a general term for the vertical main of a system of soil, waste, or vent piping.

■ solar

1. upper living room of medieval house or cattle, often over the hall.

2. upper living room , often over the great hall; the lord's private living room.

■ **solder**

to join two metal surfaces together by use of a melted metal alloy.

■ **sole plate**

bottom horizontal member of a frame wall.

■ **solid bridging**

a solid member placed between adjacent floor joists near the centre of the span to prevent joists from twisting.

■ **sorting**

segregation of sawn wood items into groups that have similar characteristics, such as thickness, species, grades, and grain patterns, and into classes for stacking or racking, such as width and length.

■ **sound knot**

a knot that is solid across its face, at least as hard as the surrounding wood, and shows no indication of decay.

■ **space frame**

see **beam grid.**

■ **spacers (shims)**

small blocks of neoprene, EPDM, silicone or other suitable material placed on each side of the glass product to provide glass centring, maintain uniform width of sealant bead and prevent excessive sealant distortion.

■ **spalling**

1. a general term applied to stonework on which the outer face is peeling off. A spall is a small piece of stone.
2. the chipping or flaking of concrete, bricks, or other masonry where improper drainage or venting and freeze/thaw cycling exists.

■ **span**

1. distance between vertical face of abutments or supports.
2. the horizontal distance between structural supports such as walls, columns, piers, beams, girders, and trusses.

■ **span (of an arch or vault)**

the horizontal distance between the two supporting members of an arch or vault. See **boss, keystone, rise, spring line.**

■ **spandrel**

1. area between top of a column or pier and the apex of the arch springing from it.
2. the roughly triangular wall space between two adjacent arches. See **arcade.**
3. triangular space between the curves of two adjacent arches and

the horizontal moulding above them.
4. the triangular shape contained by the side of an arch, a horizontal line drawn through its crown, and a vertical line on the end of the span.

■ **sparge line**

a steam pipe that has a series of holes in it.

■ **specific gravity**

the ratio of the density of wood to the density of water at 4 C. Specific gravity of wood is usually based on green volume and oven-dry weight, in which case it is known as basic specific gravity.

■ **specification**

detailed written instructions which, when clear and concise, explain each phase of work to be done.

■ **spina**

the centre strip running down the middle of a circus.

■ **spindlework**

woodwork featuring turned, curved pieces. Also called spoolwork.

■ **spiral staircase**

a staircase whose steps wind around a central, vertical axis.

■ **spire**

1. a tall, tapering, acutely pointed roof to a tower, as in the top of a steeple.
2. an elongated, pointed structure which rises from a tower, turret, or roof. Compare with pinnacle

■ **spire light**

a vertical opening in a stone spire, window-shaped, but not glazed.

■ **splash block**

a small masonry block laid with the top close to the ground surface to receive roof drainage from downspouts and to carry it away from the building.

■ **splay**

chamfer, or sloping face.

■ **splice**

to join the ends of timber elements together.

■ **split**

a defect that occurs when tensile stresses cause the wood fibres to separate and form cracks. Splits are cracks that extend through a piece.

■ **splitting**

the formation of long cracks completely through a membrane. Splits are frequently associated with lack of allowance for expansion stresses. They can also be a result of deck deflection or change in deck direction.

■ **spring**

1. level at which the springers (voussoirs) of an arch rise from their supports.
2. a longitudinal curvature of the edge of a piece of timber, not affecting the face.

■ **spring line (of an arch or a vault)**

the point or line at which an arch or vault begins to curve. See **arch, rise, span.**

■ **springer**

the lowest voussoir on each side of an arch. It is where the vertical support for the arch terminates and the curve of the arch begins. See **arch, keystone, voussoir.**

■ **springer**

horizontal voussoir at start of arch, also known as 'skew backs.'

■ **springing**

support point or origin.

■ **springing line**

level at which the arch springs from its support.

■ **spud**

the removal of gravel or heavy accumulations of bitumen from roof membranes by means of chipping or scraping.

■ **square**

a unit of measure, e.g., 100 square feet, usually applied to roofing material. Sidewall coverings are sometimes packed to cover 100 square feet and are sold on that basis.

■ **squinch**

1. an arch, or a system of concentrically wider and gradually projecting arches, placed at the corners of a square base to act as the transition to a circular dome placed on the base. Contrast with pendentive.
2. an arch which spans the angle formed by two walls meeting. Usually to carry a dome, a form which evolved into the pendentive.

■ **squint**

observation hole in wall or room.

■ **stability**

stability is best defined as the opposite of instability, which is the occurrence of large structural deformations which are not the result of material failure.

■ **stack**

a number or racks positioned one above the other and separated by bearers or gluts. Top - Any cover that protects or restrains the top rows of boards of a stack Weight - A stack top that significantly restrains the timber in the top racks of the stack. They are often a piece of flat steel or a pre-cast concrete slab the same width and length as the rack.

■ **stack vent**

also called a waste vent or soil vent, it is the extension of a soil or waste stack above the highest horizontal drain connected to the stack.

stadia

from the Greek 'stadion', which is both, the place for watching footraces, and the unit of measure like (200 meters). The ancient Greek outdoor structure used for footraces was most often built into a hillside or sloped area to provide seating for the spectators. Long and narrow in shape, the dirt track had markers for the runners in a marble strip of pavement at both ends.

stage

in western (not Orthodox) churches where worship is theatrical and the congregation functions as mainly as audience, the architect often enlarges the chancel to accommodate performances and calls it a 'stage,' as in a theatre.

stain

1. a discoloration in wood that may be caused by microorganisms, metal, or chemicals. The term also applies to materials used to impart colours to wood. Blue – a bluish or greyish discoloration in the sapwood caused by the growth of certain dark-coloured fungi. Sap - a discoloration in the sapwood caused by the growth of fungi. Sapstain is often blue but can also be red, purple and other colours.

2. a form of oil paint, very thin in consistency, intended for colouring wood with rough surfaces, such as shingles, without forming a coating of significant thickness or gloss.

stair carriage

supporting member for stair treads. Usually a 2-inch plank notched to receive the treads; sometimes called a 'rough horse.'

standing seam

a type of joint often used on metal roofs.

static load

the total amount of permanent non moving weight that is applied to given surface areas.

statically determinate

a statically determinate structure is one where there is only one distribution of internal forces and reactions which satisfies equilibrium. In a statically determinate structure, internal forces and reactions can be determined by considering nothing more than equations of equilibrium.

statically equivalent

two force systems are statically equivalent when their resultants are equal. Physically, this means that the force systems tend to impart the same motion when applied to an object; note that the distribution of resulting internal forces in the object may be different.

statically indeterminate

a statically indeterminate structure is one where there is more than one distribution of internal forces and/or reactions which satisfies equilibrium.

(Sound Transmission Class) STC

a single number rating derived from individual transmission losses at specified test frequencies. It is used for interior walls, ceilings and floors.

steam

the gaseous form of water at or above the boiling point. Saturated - Steam at 100°C and atmospheric pressure.

steaming treatment

a treatment sometimes carried out before commencing a drying schedule. The timber is subjected to live steam. See **reconditioning.**

steel trowel

tool used for non-porous smooth finishes of concrete. It is a flat steel tool used to spread and smooth plaster, mortar or concrete. Pointing trowels are small enough to be used in places where larger trowels will not fit. The pointing trowel has a point. The common trowel has a rectangular blade attached to a handle. For smooth finish, use trowel when concrete begins to stiffen.

stele

vertically standing gravestones.

step flashing

individual small pieces of metal flashing material used to flash around chimneys, dormers, and such projections along the slope of a roof. The individual pieces are overlapped and stepped up the vertical surface.

stepped

recessed in a series of ledges.

steyned

lined (like in a well).

sticker

synonymous with rack stick. Alignment - The placement of rack sticks in a rack of timber or other wood products so that they form vertical tiers. Mark - Indentation or compression of the timber or other wood product by the rack stick when the load above is too great for the bearing area. Sticker marks or sticker stain also refers to light areas under the rack stick that form as the rest of the timber darkens.

stiffener

all elements used to support or stiffen the slender webs of box and I-shaped beams and to enhance compressive capability of webs at support points or points of high transverse loads.

■ **stiff-leaf**

characteristic of early English period work, carving featuring foliage with stiff stems and lobed leaves.

■ **stiffness**

this is a general term which may be applied to materials or structures. When a force is applied to a structure, there is a displacement in the direction of the force; stiffness is the ratio of the force divided by the displacement. High stiffness means that a large force produces a small displacement. When discussing the stiffness of a material, the concept is the same, except that stress substitutes for force, and strain substitutes for displacement; see modulus of elasticity.

■ **stile**

the side frame members of a door or window (not the jamb).

■ **stitch bolt**

a long bolt through laminated timber that holds the laminations together.

■ **(Sound Transmission Loss) STL**

the reduction of the amount of sound energy passing through a wall, floor, roof, etc. It is related to the specific frequency at which it is measured and it is expressed in decibels. Also called 'Transmission Loss.'

■ **stoa**

1. (porticus) building having its roof supported by one or more rows of columns parallel to the rear wall; often a market building.
2. long colonnaded structure with a wall on one side, where people traditionally met to talk and conduct business.
3. a long, columned building used as a meeting place and shelter in ancient Greece that was usually in an Agora.
4. the long and narrow ancient Greek structure that was used for offices and shops at the agora. The enclosed space was only one office in depth, but the entire front of the building provided a wide covered porch for merchants or a convenient place to get out of the rain. Stoas were most often two stories in height.

■ **stockade**

solid fence of heavy timbers.

■ **stone/stonework**

one of the earliest and the best of all building materials, durable and much imitated in other materials, it can be worked to achieve great artistic quality, and used for floors, walls and roofs. Stone is something which can be reasonably easily handled, rock is a large mass of stone.

■ **stool**

a flat molding fitted over the window sill between jambs and contacting the bottom rail of the lower sash.

■ **storm door**

a panel or sash door placed on the outside of an existing door to provide additional protection from the elements.

■ storm window

a glazed panel or sash placed on the inside or outside of an existing sash or window as additional protection against the elements.

■ story

that part of a building between any floor and the floor or roof next above.

■ straight grained

timber in which the fibres run parallel to the axis of a piece.

■ strain

the intensity of deformation at a point in an object. See normal strain and shear strain.

■ strength

a very general term that may be applied to a material or a structure. In a material, strength refers to a level of stress at which there is a significant change in the state of the material, e.g., yielding or rupture. In a structure, strength refers to a level of level of loading which produces a significant change in the state of the structure, e.g., inelastic deformations, buckling, or collapse.

■ strength group

species of timber are classified into groups according to mechanical properties of the wood of that species and AS 2878, Timbers - Classification into Strength Group. There are seven strength groups for unseasoned timber (S1 the strongest to S7 the weakest) and eight for seasoned timber (SD 1 the strongest to SD 8 the weakest.)

■ stress

the intensity of internal force acting at a point in an object. Stress is measured in units of force per area. See **shear stress and normal stress.**

■ stress resultant

a system of forces which is statically equivalent to a stress distribution over an area.

■ striking off

the operation of smoothing off excess compound or sealant at sight line when applying same around lites or panels.

■ string (or stringer)

a timber or other support for cross members in floors or ceilings. In stairs, the support on which the stair treads rest; also stringboard.

■ string line

a nylon line usually strung tightly between supports to indicate both direction and elevation, used in checking grades or deviations in slopes or rises. Used in landscaping to level the ground.

■ stringcourse

a continuous projecting horizontal band set in the surface of a wall and usually molded.

■ stringer

a beam that joins the top of columns and supports the cross members in floors and ceilings. An inclined member that supports the treads of a stair. A deck element in timber bridges that supports transverse deck planks and runs parallel to the beam span.

strip flooring

wood flooring consisting of narrow, matched strips.

structural model

an idealisation for analysis purposes of a real or conceived structure. A structural model includes boundaries limiting the scope of the analysis. Supports occur at these boundaries, representing things which hold the structure in place.

structural silicone glazing

the use of a silicone sealant for the structural transfer of loads from the glass to its perimeter support system and retention of the glass in the opening.

structural timber

timber to be used in construction where its strength is the controlling element in its selection and use.

strut

a structural timber resisting compressive forces along the grain.

stucco

a sturdy type of plaster used on exterior walls; often spread in a decorative pattern.

stud

one of a series of vertical framing timbers used as a supporting element in a wall or partition.

stylobate

the top step of the crepidoma.

subceontractor

a contractor who specialises in a particular trade such as waterproofing.

subfloor

1. boards or plywood laid on joists over which a finish floor is to be laid.
2. that which is depicted on an architectural drawing or other document. It can represent a design, an exercise, or an architectural work, built or unbuilt.

sub-rough

that part of a building's plumbing system that is done before the cement is poured.

substrate

a part or substance which lies below and supports another.

suburban

the meaning of 'sub' is, falling nearly in the category of, that is, not quite urban; missing some of the important components to be defined as urban. See **urban.**

sudatorium

sweat room, steam room of a Roman bath complex.

summa cavea

Latin: highest or summit theatre seating, highest tier of cavea seating; used by less distinguished audience members.

super heat

the heat in steam in excess of the amount of heat in saturated steam at a given pressure.

■ support

a support contributes to keeping a structure in place by restraining one or more degrees of freedom. In a structural model, supports represent boundary entities which are not included in the model itself, e.g., foundations, abutments, or the earth itself. For each restrained translation degree of freedom at a support, there is a corresponding reaction force; for each restrained rotation degree of freedom, there is a reaction moment.

■ surface force

a force applied to the surface of an object.

■ suspended ceiling

a ceiling system supported by hanging it from the overhead structural framing.

■ sustainable

a resource or system that meets present needs without compromising those of future generations. Example a continuously maintained forest where mature trees are harvested and new trees are replanted to filter pollutants and provide continued resources and products for future generations.

■ sway bracing

bracing members required to resists the transverse movement of a structural element.

■ swelling

an increase in the dimensions of wood resulting from an increase in moisture content. Swelling occurs tangentially, radially, and, to a lesser extent, longitudinally.

■ swirl figure

a figure caused by irregular grain in the region of the knot.

■ symbolise

to use a symbol to represent something.

■ system of forces

one or more forces and/or moments acting simultaneously.

■ taberna

a small shop.

■ tablinum

a central room off the atrium of a Roman house. Used as master bedroom.

■ tail beam

a relatively short beam or joist supported in a wall on one end and by a header at the other.

■ tangential

coincident with a tangent at the circumference of a tree or log, or parallel to such a tangent. In practice, it often means roughly coincident with a growth ring.

■ taper

reducing gradually in width or diameter.

■ taping

applying joint tape over embedding compound in the process of joint treatment of drywall.

■ tau cross

plain T cross with equal limbs.

■ **taverna**

a small restaurant serving traditional Greek food that is generally less expensive and more authentic than a restaurant.

■ **tear-off**

in roofing, a term used to describe the complete removal of the built up roof membrane and insulation down to and exposing the roof deck.

■ **telchines**

according to mythology, Telchines were born of the sea and were the first ones to inhabit Rhodes. They are particularly known as metallurgists and inventive craftsmen. It is said that they were the first ones to finely work iron and bronze and made many wonderful works such as Cronus' sickle and Poseidon's trident.

■ **temenos**

sacred area surrounding a temple; temple precinct, often walled off from surroundings.

■ **temple**

1. in Imperial Rome, the structure used for religious ritual of the priests, and either rectangular or round in plan. The earlier rectangular plan temples have bearing walls. The round Pantheon employs an arcuated system for enclosing the space. Both forms stood on podiums and were meant to be approached only from the front.
2. the ancient Greek structure built to shelter the god statue, and the focus of religious worship. Thus, the Parthenon in Athens is the structure that was built to shelter the 40 foot tall ivory and gold statue of Athena Parthenos.

■ **tension**

a state or condition of being pulled or stretched by a force.

■ **tepidarium**

warm bath of a Roman bath complex.

■ **termite shield**

a shield, usually of noncorrodible metal, placed in or on a foundation wall or other mass of masonry or around pipes to prevent passage of termites.

■ **termites**

whitish ant-like social insect of the order Isoptera found in warm and tropical regions. Some species feed on wood, causing damage to furniture, buildings, and trees.

■ **terneplate**

sheet iron or steel coated with an alloy of lead and tin.

■ **terracotta**

molded, fired and glazed clay units used as an exterior finish material.

■ **tessera (plural tesserae)**

small piece of stone, glass, etc. used in making a mosaic.• See **mosaic.**

■ **tetrakionia**

a monument with four architectural elements placed at the crossing of two major street intersections in a Roman town or city, as at Palmyra.

tetrapylon

also known as a quadrifronic arch. An arch monument at a major street intersection which has two vaults so people may pass through in all directions, as at the ruined arch at Lepcis Magna.

tetrastoon

of Greek origin referring to 'four rows of columns'; also a meeting place or public square

tetrastyle temple

having a Portico of four columns at either end.

texture

characteristic determined by the size and quality of the wood elements. Descriptive terms include fine, medium, uniform, even, uneven, coarse.

texture paint

one which may be manipulated by brush, trowel or other to give various patterns.

the decorated style

the second of the three distinctive architectural styles of England's cathedrals, the first being Early English, the later, Perpendicular. A generalised date for the Decorated era is the middle thirteenth to the middle fourteenth centuries. It is within this period that the more distinctive features of English Gothic emerge, leaving behind evident transitional links with the Romanesque. Westminster Abbey is an example of construction during this era.

the orders

order is a good term in this context, it implies both an acceptable organisation of component parts and a satisfying relationship between them. A colossal or giant order is any order, the columns of which extend through more than one floor.

theatre

1. the ancient Roman building type used for dramatic performance or entertainment. Unlike the Greek theatre, the building is free standing, the wall behind the stage is much higher and the seating area may be covered. Picture shows Roman theatre, Merida, Spain.
2. in ancient Greece, going to the theatre was a celebration of community, and the dramas and comedies portrayed moral virtue and vice. The structure was built into a hillside and the wall behind the stage structure was relatively low, so that the audience could, by looking over the actors heads, view the entire polis.

theatron

Greek: from (theasthai, to see); originally referred to the 'watching space' of the Greek theatre, but later became synonymous with the entire auditorium consisting of the spaces for both the audience as well as the performance.

thermal insulation

any material high in resistance to heat transmission that, when placed in the walls, ceiling, or floors of a structure, will reduce the rate of heat flow.

thermal movement

the measured amount of dimensional change that a material exhibits as it is warmed or cooled.

thermal shock

the stress built up by sudden and appreciable changes in temperature.

thermoplastic material

solid material which is softened by increasing temperatures and hardened by decreasing temperatures.

tholos

in ancient Greek architecture, this structure may have been a temple, a tomb, or the building for keeping the weights and measures. It is round in plan, with columns at the perimeter.
At Delphi, the tholos is located in a sacred precinct and dedicated to Athena. In Athens, the tholos is located on the agora.

threshold

a strip of wood or metal with beveled edges used over the finish floor and the sill of exterior doors.

thrust

the outward force exerted by an arch or a vault that must be counterbalanced by buttresses.

thru-wall flashing

flashing extended completely through a masonry wall. Designed and applied in combination with counter-flashings, to prevent water which may enter the wall above from proceeding downward in the wall or into the roof deck or roofing system.

THW

moisture and heat resistant thermoplastic conductor. It is flame retardant, moisture and heat resistant and can be used in dry or wet locations.

thymele

Greek: also 'bema'; platform in the orchestra, next to the altar of Dionysus, both called the thymele; it is suggested that the leader of the chorus used the thymele as a platform during dialogues between the chorus leader (coryphaios) and the chorus.

thyromata

doors and their frames which pierce the facade of the skene or episkenion In the Hellenistic theatre; (Greek: 'a room with doors to it, a chamber' or 'a door with posts and frame'.)

thyromata wall

wall that contains thyromata or openings; also refers to the Greek proskenion.

tie

a structural member resisting tension forces along the grain.

tied arch

an arch tied at the base with a tension member.

tie-in

in roofing, a term used to describe the joining of a new roof with the old.

tierceron

a major rib in a complex rib vault. Tiercerons spring from the main springers. See **rib vault, springer Other types of ribs lierne, ridge, diagonal, transverse.**

■ **tilt-up wall**

cast concrete units which are preformed which, when cured, are tilted

■ **timber**

a general term for natural or sawn wood in a form suitable for building or structural purposes.

■ **timbers**

yard lumber 5 or more inches in least dimension. Includes beams, stringers, posts, caps, sills, girders, and purlins.

■ **tin ceiling**

ceiling constructed of tiles that are pressed from tin.

■ **tinted glass**

glass with colorants added to the basic glass batch that give the glass colour as well as light and heat-reducing capabilities. The colour extends throughout the thickness of the glass.

■ **toe bead**

sealant applied at the intersection of the outboard glazing stop and the bottom of the glazing channel; must be sized to also provide a seal to the edge of the glass.

■ **toenailing**

to drive a nail at a slant with the initial surface in order to permit it to penetrate into a second member.

■ **tongue & groove**

a type of flooring where the tongue of one board is joined to the groove of another board.

■ **tongue and groove joint**

a joint where a ridge or tongue in one piece fits a matching groove in the other.

■ **tooling**

the operation of pressing in and striking a sealant in a joint to press the sealant against the sides of a joint and secure good adhesion; the finishing off of the surface of a sealant in a joint so that it is flush with the surface.

■ **tooth-in**

stones removed (or omitted) to allow another wall to be bonded into it.

■ **top mopping**

the finished mopping of hot bitumen on a built-up roof.

■ **top plate**

top horizontal member of a frame wall.

■ **torching**

applying direct flame to a membrane for the purpose of melting, heating or adhering.

■ **toughness**

a quality of wood which permits the material to absorb a relatively large amount of energy, to withstand repeated shocks, and to undergo considerable deformation before breaking.

■ **tracery**

1. ornament of ribs, bars, etc., in panels or screens, as in the upper part of a Gothic window.
2. intersecting ribwork in upper part of window.
3. branching, ornamental stonework, generally in a window, where it supports the glass; particularly characteristic of Gothic architecture.
4. stonework patterns in a window, allowing for greater size and strength.
5. curvilinear decoration used in windows, primarily Gothic style lancet windows.
6. the thin stone supporting pieces in a gothic window, characterised by interlacing or branching forms.

■ **tracheid**

the elongated cells that constitute the greater part of the structure of the softwoods; also present but uncommon in some hardwoods.

■ **trade names**

the accepted regional names given to particular species by industry.

■ **trancept**

1. the arm of the cruciform church at right-angles to the nave.
2. the parts of the church perpendicular to the main axis of the church, to the North and South. May be off the Crossing, or in other places (Lincoln has eastern trancepts, Ely has Western trancepts.)
3. a rectangular area which cuts across the main axis of a basilica-type building and projects beyond it. The transept gives a basilica the shape of a Latin cross and usually serves to separate the main area of the building from an apse at the end. See **other parts of a church ambulatory, apse, choir, crossing, east end, nave, west end.**
4. the crossing arms in a church with a Latin cross plan.

■ **transit**

a surveyors instrument used by builders to establish points and elevations both vertically and horizontally. It can be used to line up stakes or to plumb walls or the angle of elevation from a horizontal plane can be measured.

■ **transitional sawn**

timbers sawn so that there are both back sawn and quarter sawn sections in the piece.

■ **translation**

motion of an object where the path of every point is a straight line.

■ **transmissibility**

the principle stating that a force has the same external effect on an object regardless of where it acts along its line of action.

■ **transom**

1. horizontal division of window; crossbar.

2. a horizontal cross member in a window.

■ **transverse**

across. A transverse section is a section across the length of a building or room.

■ **transverse arch**

supporting arch which runs across the vault from side to side, dividing the bays. it usually projects down from the surface of the vault. Compare with transverse rib.

■ **transverse rib**

the projecting bands which mark the transverse arches of a rib vault. See **rib vault, springer.** Other types of ribs lierne, ridge, diagonal, tierceron.

■ **transverse vaulting**

the use of ribs or arches set at right angles from the corners of a structure.

■ **tread**

the horizontal platform of a stair.

■ **trefoil**

1. three-lobed.
2. an ornamental form which has three lobes or foils. Compare with cinqfoil, quatrefoil.
3. three-lobed infilling for a circle or arch-head.

■ **tremie**

a tube with removable sections and a funnel at the top used in concrete application. The bottom is kept beneath the surface of the concrete and raised as the form is filled and is used to pour concrete underwater.

■ **triangulation**

joining structural members together so that they form a rigid triangle

■ **tribunal**

in a Roman theatre, the tribunal was a raised platform for the seat of judgment of the praetor; platforms for this seat of honour in theatre would normally be above the aditus maximus (above the two side entrances to the orchestra on the extreme left and right of the caveat.)

■ **tribunalia**

Roman seat of judgment; in the theatre, a seat of honour placed on the tribunal or platform above the aditus maximus (side entrance to the orchestra between the pulpitum and the cavea); performers or victors of gladiatorial games would receive recognition from the praetor who sat in this seat.

■ **tribune**

a vaulted gallery which forms or covers the ceiling of an isle.

■ **tribune or gallery**

an upper story over the aisle which opens onto the nave or choir. It corresponds in length and width to the dimensions of the aisle below it. Contrast with triforium. See **aisle, clerestory.**

triceron ribs

pairs of ribs springing from the same place as the principal ribs but meeting obliquely instead of carrying over to the other side of the vault in a continuous line.

triceron vault

a vault incorporating Triceron ribs.

triclinium

dining area of a Roman house (domus), consisting of three couch like platforms around the three sides of the room upon which diners would recline.

triforium

an arcaded wall passage, extending around a church between the ground floor arcade and the clerestory.

triforium or triforium passage

a narrow passage in the thickness of the wall with arches opening onto the nave. It may occur at the level of the clerestory windows, or it may be located as a separate level below the clerestory. It may itself have an outer wall of glass rather than stone. Contrast with gallery or tribune See **clerestory.**

triglyph

1. the blocks with vertical grooves separating the metopes in a Doric frieze. Said to represent beam ends.

2. a decorative element of the Doric Frieze that alternates with the Metopes and is formed by three grooves, or glyphs.

trim

the finish materials in a building, such as moldings applied around openings (window trim, door trim) or at the floor and ceiling of rooms (baseboard, cornice, and other moldings.)

trimmer

the structural member on the side of a framed rough opening to narrow or stiffen the opening. Also the shortened stud (jack stud) which supports a header in a door or window opening.

trimmer

a beam or joist to which a header is nailed in framing for a chimney, stairway, or other opening.

trireme

1. fast warship powered by up to 170 oarsmen positioned over three levels on either side of the hull. The trireme was the most widely used warship in ancient Greece. Alight hull ballasted with blocks of stone in the hold, had three decks which housed the banks of oarsmen, while the bridge accommodated the troops to be landed or, more often,

ready to board enemy ships after they have been rammed. At the prow was a pointed ram strengthened with metal, which could sink enemy ships.

There were often eyes painted on the prow.

2. an ancient Greek ship with three rows of oars on each side.

trumeau

vertical architectural member between the leaves of a doorway. Trumeaus were often highly decorated. See **jamb, trumeau figure.**

trumeau figure

statue decorating a trumeau. Usually this was a human figure, very often a religious personage. See **jamb figures, trumeau.**

truss

1. a timber frame used to support the roof over the great hall.

2. a frame or jointed structure designed to act as a beam of long span, while each member is usually subjected to longitudinal stress only, either tension or compression.

3. a frame of members in the same plane joined only at their end and all interconnected to form triangles. Primary stresses are axial so that if loads are applied at the joints, the stress in each member is in the direction of its length.

trussed arch

an arch where the main member is made up of elements arranged as a truss.

trussed beam

a timber beam reinforced with a trussed metal tension rod.

tuck pointing

the repair of a mortar joint. First the joint is cleaned of loose debris, then new mortar of the same composition of the original is added back into the joint.

tudor

a style of English architecture prevalent during the reigns of the Tudors (1485- 1558), transitional between Gothic and Palladian, with emphasis on privacy and interiors.

tufa

cellular rock; porous limestone.

turning bridge

a drawbridge that pivots in the middle.

turpentine

a volatile oil used as a thinner in paints and as a solvent in varnishes. Chemically, it is a mixture of terpenes.

turret

1. a small tower, usually starting at some distance from the ground, attached to a building such as a castle or fortress.

3. small tower, round or polygonal; usually a lookout.

5. a small, often ornamental tower projecting from a building, usually at a corner.

turret, tourelle

a small tower, usually corbelled, at the corner of a building and extending above it.

tuscan

confined mainly to the north of Italy, it was employed by the Romans but replaced by the Doric. Very plain, the columns are not fluted, and in height it is usually around seven diameters.

tuscan order

a Roman order resembling the Doric without a fluted shaft.

TW

moisture-resistant thermoplastic conductor that can be used in dry or wet locations and has no outer covering and is not heat-resistant.

twentieth century commercial

a functional building style with modest ornamentation. Most of these building are four to five stories or less, constructed of brick, and uses as store fronts for retail or service establishments.

twist

a spiral distortion along the length of a piece of timber.

twisted ribbon

an ornamental motif of thin, continuous bands arranged in a rectilinear fashion, and represented as if the bands were three dimensional. See **other repetitive decorative motifs**

two-part sealant

a product composed of a base and curing agent or accelerator, necessarily packages in two separate containers which are uniformly mixed just prior to use.

tympanum

1. space between lintel and arch over doorway.
2. triangular surface bounded by the mouldings of a pediment; also the space, often carved, between the lintel and arch of a Gothic doorway.
3. the region between the lintel and the arch over a doorway, often decorated with relief work.
4. the section atop the lintel of a portal or doorway, enclosed by an arch, often featuring significant sculpture work. Image at right: Tympanum within the west portal of Notre Dame de Chartres, France.

undercoat

a coating applied prior to the finishing or top coats of a paint job. It may be the first of two or the second of three coats. In some usage of the word it may, become synonymous with priming coat.

underlayment

a material placed under finish coverings, such as flooring, or shingles, to provide a smooth, even surface for applying the finish.

uprights

vertical members supporting the sides of a trench.

urban

in architecture, the functions and forms of the city; anything related to, or characteristic of, the city.

u-value

a measure of air-to-heat transmission (loss or gain) due to the thermal conductance and the difference in indoor and outdoor temperatures. As the U-value decreases, so does the amount of heat that is transferred through the glazing material. The lower the U-value, the more restrictive the fenestration product is to heat transfer. Reciprocal of R-value.

valley

the internal angle formed by the junction of two sloping sides of a roof.

valley rafter

a rafter that forms the intersection of an internal roof angle. The valley rafter is normally made of double 2-inch-thick members.

valva regia

(also aula regia) main, central entrance to the stage in the Hellenistic theatre; also known as the 'king's or royal door'; corresponds to the porta reggia of the Roman theatre.

valve

a device to stop, start or regulate the flow of liquid or gas through or from piping.

vapour

the gaseous form of any substance.

vapour barrier

1. a membrane which is placed between the insulation and the roof deck to retard water vapour in the building from entering the insulation and condensing into liquid water.
2. material used to retard the movement of water vapour into walls and prevent condensation in them. Usually considered as having a perm value of less than 1.0. Applied separately over the warm side of exposed walls or as a part of batt or blanket insulation.
3. in kiln drying, a material with high resistance to vapour movement that is applied to the surfaces of a dry kiln to prevent moisture migration.

varnish

a thickened preparation of drying oil and resin suitable for spreading on surfaces to form continuous, transparent coatings, or for mixing with pigments to make enamels.

vault

1. an arched brick or stone ceiling or roof. The simplest form is the barrel vault, a single continuous arch; the groined vault consists of two barrel vaults joined at right angles; a ribbed vault has diagonal

arches projecting from the surface.
2. stone roofing.
3. a roof or ceiling built in stone, brick or concrete, as opposed to wood.
4. in all architecture; an arched structure of stone or masonry forming a ceiling.

vehicle

the liquid portion of a finishing material; it consists of the binder (non-volatile) and volatile thinners.

veining

in roofing, the characteristic lines or 'stretch marks' which develop during the aging process of soft bitumens.

velum

also ' velarium' (Latin: sail or fabric awning) fabric awning used to shade audience in Roman cavea; also a sail, especially the large square mainsail.

veneer

1. a decorative covering of brick, wood, stone, or other material over rough construction, used to simulate more substantial or expensive construction.
2. thin sheets of wood made by rotary cutting or slicing of a log.

veneering

facing a substrate with a thin layer of ornamental wood.

vent

in kiln drying, an opening in the kiln roof or wall that can be opened and closed to control the humidity in the kiln.

vent pipe

a vertical pipe of relatively small dimensions which protrudes through a roof to provide for the ventilation of gasses.

vent stack

a vertical vent pipe installed for the purpose of providing circulation of air to and from any part of a drainage system.

vent system

in plumbing, a system to provide a flow of air to or from a drainage system or to provide circulation of air within such system to protect traps seals from siphonage and back pressure.

ventilator

device installed on the roof for the purpose of ventilating the interior of the building.

venting

the process of installing roof vents in a roof assembly to relieve vapour pressure; The process of water in the insulation course of the roof assembly evaporating and exiting via the roof vents.

veranda

a roofed area attached to the side of a structure and supported by columns or pillars.

verge board

also known as a bargeboard or gableboard. A board that covers the gable end of a roof.

■ vermiculated or vermiculation

a decorative motif characterised by shallow channels that appear to have been made by worms. Usually found as a decorative surface on stone masonry.

■ vermiculite

an aggregate somewhat similar to perlite that is used as an aggregate in lightweight roof decks and deck fills. It is formed from mica, a hydrous silicate with the ability of expanding on heating to form lightweight material with insulation quality. Used as bulk insulation and also as aggregate in insulating and acoustical plaster and in insulating concrete.

■ vernacular

1. a style or form of building developed not by architects but by local custom, and based on the use of regional materials, techniques, and forms.
2. a wood to describe simple architecture that is often a mix of styles or has no particular style that can be attributed to it.

■ versurae

architectural parts of the theatron flanking the stage of a Roman theatre; Roman equivalent to the Greek paraskenion; also see itinera versurarum.

■ vertically laminated timber

laminated timber designed to resist bending loads applied parallel to the wide face of the laminations. For vertical loads, this means that the wide face runs vertically.

■ vesica

a pointed oval composed of sections of two intersecting circles.

■ vessels

tube-like structure of indeterminate length in hardwoods which carry water and nutrients from the roots.

■ via venatorium

Latin: road or way of the hunter, a complex of hallways and rooms which housed animals and equipment.

■ villa

a country house for the ancient Romans, typically of one story with a central atrium or courtyard. This term is also applied to many of the houses along the seawall in Pompeii and Ercolano (Herculaneum) because these cities were seaside resorts for wealthy Romans.

■ visible light transmittance

the percentage of visible light (390 to 770) nanometers) within the solar spectrum that is transmitted through glass.

■ visual mock-up

small scale demonstration of a finished construction product.

■ **vitrified**

material reduced to glass by extreme heat.

■ **VOC**

Volatile Organic Compound. A highly evaporative, carbon-based chemical substance, which produces noxious fumes; found in many paints, caulks, stains, and adhesives.

■ **volatile thinner**

a liquid that evaporates readily and is used to thin or reduce the consistency of finishes without altering the relative volumes of pigment and non-volatile vehicles.

■ **volume, green**

the volume of wood determined from measurements made while the entire piece of wood is above the fibre saturation point, about 30% moisture content.

■ **volumes**

volumes are bound albums and sketchbooks, the contents of which may or may not vary in the subjects depicted, technique, and media.

■ **volute**

1. spiral scroll at each corner of an Ionic or Corinthian capital.
2. a spiral scroll, found on the capital of the ionic order. The centre is often referred to as the 'eye'.

■ **vomitoria**

theatre entrances or exits for audience; vaulted passageways leading to or from the cavea; also **see aditus**

■ **voussoir**

1. wedge-shaped stones in arch.
2. one of the wedge-shaped stones used in constructing an arch.
3. wedged shaped masonry used to create an arch or used to define a lintel or door header.

■ **wagon roof**

1. a curved wooden rafter roof, such as at South well.
2. a ceiling of curved wooden beams, often intersected in intricate designs.

■ **wainscoting**

wood panelling or other material applied to the lower portion of an interior wall.

■ **walkways**

designated areas for foot traffic.

■ **wall walk**

a passage along the castle wall.

■ **wall-plate**

horizontal roof-timber on wall-top.

■ **wall-stair**

staircase built into the thickness of a wall.

■ **wane**

the absence of wood on any face or edge of a piece of timber, leaving exposed the original under bark surface with or without bark.

waney edge/waney timber

boards or pieces of timber which, instead of being cut square, show the original curve of the log from which they are cut.

want

the absence of wood, other than wane, from the arris or surface of a piece of timber.

warp

any variation from a true and plane surface. It includes bow, cup and twist and is often caused by irregular seasoning.

warp restraint

in drying timber and other wood products, the application of external loads to a rack, stack or pack to prevent or reduce warp.

water repellent coating

transparent coating or sealer applied to the surface of concrete and masonry surfaces to repel water.

water repellent

a liquid that penetrates wood which, after drying, materially retards changes in moisture content and in dimensions without adversely altering the desirable properties of wood.

water repellent preservative

a liquid designed to penetrate into wood and impart water repellency and a moderate preservative protection. It is used for millwork, such as sash and frames, and is usually applied by dipping.

water-cement ratio

the strength of a concrete mixture depends on the water cement ratio. The water and cement form a paste. If the paste is made with more water, the concrete becomes weaker. Traditionally, concrete mixes have been identified in terms of the ratio of cement to fine aggregate to coarse aggregate. For example, the ratio 1:2:4 refers to a mix which consists of 1 cu. ft. of cement, 2 cu. ft. of sand and 4 cu. ft. of gravel. Cement and water are the two chemically active elements in concrete and when combined, form a paste or glue which coats and surrounds the particles of aggregate and upon hardening binds the entire mass together.

water-leaf

plain broad leaf moulding.

waterproofing

the process where a building component is made totally resistant to the passage of water and/or water vapour.

wattle

a mat of woven (willow) sticks and weeds; used in wall and dike construction.

■ **wave**

sinuous moulding.

■ **wavy figure**

markings in the form of waves or undulations. Figures with large undulations are described as 'wavy', while others with small, irregular undulations are 'curly', and those with small, regular undulations are 'fiddle back'.

■ **weather vane**

a decorative plate that is mounted on a rod to move freely to indicate wind direction.

■ **weatherboard**

boards that cover external surfaces and overlap to keep out the rain.

■ **weathering**

1. sloping surface to throw off rainwater.
2.
3. the mechanical or chemical disintegration and discolouration of the surface of wood caused by exposure to light, the action of dust and sand carried by winds, and the alternate shrinking and swelling of the surface fibres with the variation in moisture content. Weathering does not include decay.

■ **weatherstrip**

narrower or jamb-width sections of thin metal or other material to prevent infiltration of air and moisture around windows and doors. Compression weather stripping prevents air infiltration, provides tension, and acts as a counter balance.

■ **web**

any transverse lateral stiffener.

■ **webbing or infilling**

the vault surface between the ribs of a rib vault. Compare with rib.

■ **weep hole**

a hole which allows for drainage of entrapped water from masonry or glazing structures.

■ **weep screed**

tool used to drain moisture from concrete.

■ **weld**

the joining of components together by fusing. In thermoplastics, refers to bonding together of the membrane using heat or solvents.

■ **west end**

the area of the church opposite the east end. The west end usually functions as the main entrance to the church. Contrast with east end See **screen facade, narthex.** Westwork.

■ **west front**

the western wall of the nave, often decorated and topped with towers.

westwork
in German Romanesque, a monumental entrance to a church consisting of porches and towers, with a chapel above.

westwork(from German westwerk)
an entrance area at the west end of a church with upper chamber and usually with a tower or towers. It is normally broader than the width of the nave and aisles. Westwork is sometimes used synonymously with narthex.

wet seal
application of an elastomeric sealant between the glass and sash to form a weather tight seal.

wicket
person-sized door set into the main gate door.

widow's walk
1. a deck on top of a flat roof usually enclosed by a balustrade, frequently made of cast iron. Widow's walks once had a practical purpose and were used frequently on seaside houses. The lady of the house could go to the roof to see which ships had arrived in the harbour. If her husbands ship never returned, she knew she was a widow, thus the name.
2. historically, a platform on a roof from which the wives of colonial New England seamen could watch for their return.

wild figure
irregular markings.

wind bracing
bracing members required to resist the forces on a structure resulting from wind pressure.

wind post
a column that stiffens a framed wall against wind loads.

wind power
wind power is generated through the use of a turbine, usually mounted on a tower. The turbine collects wind energy and converts it to electricity which is transferred to your houses breaker panel, allowing you to rely on your existing utility power supply as only a backup.

wind uplift
the upward force exerted by wind travelling across a roof.

wing-wall
wall down slope of motte to protect stairway.

wire drawn brick
clay that has been scored by wire prior to being fired at a high temperature.

wood filler
a heavily pigmented preparation used for fining and levelling off the pores in open-pored woods.

wood rays
strips of cells extending radially within a tree and varying in height from a few cells in some species to 4 inches or more in oak. The rays serve primarily to store food and to transport it horizontally in the tree.

wood fibre plaster

consists of calcified gypsum integrally mixed with selected coarse cellulose fibres which provide bulk and greater coverage. It is formulated to produce high-strength base coats for use in highly fire-resistant ceiling assemblies.

workability

the degree of ease and smoothness of cut obtainable with hand or machine tools.

work-life

the time during which a curing sealant remains suitable for use after being mixed with a catalyst.

xeriscape

quality, low-maintenance landscaping that conserves water and protects the environment by using mulch, soil analysis, and appropriate plant selection. Especially beneficial in drought-ridden areas.

yard lumber

lumber of those grades, sizes, and patterns which are generally intended for ordinary construction, such as framework and rough coverage of houses.

yett

iron lattice gate.

yield strain

a material deformed beyond its yield strain, no longer exhibits linear elastic behaviour. See **yield stress.**

yield stress

a material loaded beyond its yield stress, no longer exhibits linear elastic behaviour. Metals, particularly mild steel, generally have a very well defined yield stress compared to other materials. Yield stress is sometimes called yield strength.

zoophorous

used to describe a frieze decorated with animal or human figures.

Notes

Notes

Notes

Other Books on

LOTUS ILLUSTRATED DICTIONARIES

1. Dictionary of New Words (New)	125/-
2. Dictionary of Veterinary Sciences (New)	125/-
3. Dictionary of Synonyms and Antonyms (New)	150/-
4. Dictionary of Idioms and Phrases (New)	150/-
5. First English Dictionary	125/-
6. Astronomy	125/-
7. Agriculture	125/-
8. Anthropology	125/-
9. Archaeology	125/-
10. Architecture	125/-
11. Art	125/-
12. Banking Finance & Accounting	125/-
13. Bio-Chemistry	125/-
14. Business Administration	125/-
15. Bio-Technology	125/-
16. Biology	125/-
17. Botany	125/-
18. Culture	125/-
19. Chemical Engg.	125/-
20. Chemistry	125/-
21. Civil Engineering	125/-
22. Computer Science	125/-
23. Commerce	125/-
24. Cooking & Food	125/-
25. Ecology	125/-
26. Economics	125/-
27. Education	125/-
28. Electrical Engineering	125/-
29. Electronic & Telecommunication	125/-
30. Environmental Studies	125/-
31. Festival	125/-
32. Geography	125/-

33. Geology	125/-
34. Genetic Engineering	125/-
35. Health & Nutrition	125/-
36. History	125/-
37. Import and Export	125/-
38. Information System Management	125/-
39. Internet	125/-
40. IT	125/-
41. Inorganic Chemistry	125/-
42. Law	125/-
43. Library & Information Science	125/-
44. Literature	125/-
45. Management	125/-
46. Mathematics	125/-
47. Marketing & Sales	125/-
48. Mass Communication	125/-
49. Mechanical Engg.	125/-
50. Medical	125/-
51. Music	125/-
52. Organic Chemistry	125/-
53. Philosophy	125/-
54. Physical Education	125/-
55. Physics	125/-
56. Psychology	125/-
57. Science	125/-
58. Sex	125/-
59. Sociology	125/-
60. Sports	125/-
61. Textile	125/-
62. Zoology	125/-

Unit No. 220, Second Floor, 4735/22,
Prakash Deep Building, Ansari Road, Darya Ganj,
New Delhi - 110002, Ph.: 32903912, 23280047, 09811594448
E-mail: lotuspress1984@gmail.com, www.lotuspress.co.in